International Management

Cases and Exercises

Charles Rarick and Arifin Angriawan

authorHOUSE®

AuthorHouse™
1663 Liberty Drive
Bloomington, IN 47403
www.authorhouse.com
Phone: 1-800-839-8640

First published by AuthorHouse   02/21/2011

ISBN: 978-1-4208-0652-6 (sc)

Printed in the United States of America

CONTENTS

PART FOUR
INTERNATIONAL STAFFING AND HRM 117

PART FIVE
SOCIAL RESPONSIBILITY 157

PREFACE

This book acts as a supplement to the traditional text in international or cross-cultural management and is considered appropriate for both undergraduate and graduate audiences. The cases and exercises can be utilized as in-class activities or assigned as homework.

The book provides a practical approach to the study of the subject, and students can apply what they have read in the textbook or learned in class to problems relevant to transnational management. A strong emphasis of the book is the importance of culture to international management issues.

The cases and exercises are organized into common themes such as cultural influences, communication and negotiation, strategy and location decisions, staffing, and ethical concerns. The cases and exercises can, however, be used in a flexible manner. The cases, especially, involve multiple areas of concern to international management and can be used at different points in a course. Instructors should feel free to use the material as they deem appropriate, regardless of the book's organization.

A particular strength of the book is the diversity of cultures found in the cases. The cases involve management and cultural issues involving countries such as Argentina, Canada, China, France, Germany, India, Israel, Japan, Mexico, Poland, Russia, Taiwan, Thailand, and African and Middle Eastern countries.

The text is based on the belief that learning is best achieved through more active student involvement in the educational process. The cases require students to think independently about complex international management issues, and the exercises attempt to internalize and reinforce basic concepts. The book makes a course in international or cross-cultural management more interesting and effective.

ABOUT THE AUTHORS

Charles A. Rarick is a professor of international business at Purdue University Calumet. Previously he was the Director of International Business in the Andreas School of Business, Barry University. He has also taught at Transylvania University, University of Kentucky, Xavier University, Northwest Missouri State University, and Brescia University, and lectured at Instituto Tecnologico y Estudios Superiores de Monterrey ITESM (Mexico), EAFIT in Colombia, the Romanian-American University in Bucharest, Asian Institute of Technology in Thailand, and International University of Business and Economics in China. Dr. Rarick received his Ph.D. from Saint Louis University and he is certified as a Senior Professional in Human Resource Management. He is also the author of *Cases and Exercises in International Business* (Prentice Hall) and *The Confucian Advantage* (Cummings and Hathaway). Dr. Rarick was a Fulbright Senior Specialist to Burma, and the 2006/2007 Fulbright Distinguished Lecturer to the Philippines.

Arifin Angriawan is an assistant professor of management in the School of Management, Purdue University Calumet in Hammond, Indiana. Dr. Angriawan received his Ph.D. degree from Southern Illinois University Carbondale. He is a member of the Academy of Management, Strategic Management Society, and the Decision Sciences Institute. He has published in several academic journals including Journal of Leadership and Organization Studies, Journal of Business Strategies, and Journal of Entrepreneurship and Innovation Management.

PART ONE

THE ROLE OF CULTURE

The cultural environment of a country is shaped by many factors includes education, values, religion, and social structure. Culture plays an important role on how an individual perceives and interprets managerial, organizational, and social realities. Thus, people from different cultural backgrounds have different perceptions and interpretations of events. The following cases provide some examples of the impacts of cultural difference on international business and management.

Cases:
Trying to do Business in Mexico, Gringo Style
Au Revoir, Mrs. Williamson
Polska PipeWorks
The Dead Sea Salt Processing
Dancing with an Elephant
An American Gaucho in Argentina

Exercises:
Who Am I?
Cross-Cultural Quiz
Ranking Cultures
Cultural Metaphors

CASE 1

TRYING TO DO BUSINESS IN MEXICO, GRINGO STYLE

ABSTRACT

This case explores the difficulties an American expatriate experiences in starting and managing an American-Mexican joint venture. Ted Dorman was selected to manage the new joint venture, and he experiences many cultural difficulties adjusting to his new assignment as he attempts to institute new policies.

Ted Dorman was looking forward to his new assignment as plant manager at a newly formed American-Mexican joint venture in Guadalajara, Mexico. The American company, Sterling Metal, produced hardware and decorative fixtures for furniture manufacturers in the United States and Mexico. The new joint venture was an attempt to lower labor costs by operating in Mexico.

Ted and the Dorman Family

Ted had worked at Sterling Metal since graduating from college with a degree in accounting. He had worked his way up in the company through accounting, and eventually shifted his career focus to production. Ted found the challenges of managing the production function very interesting, and he was successful in this area. His position at the new company, SterMexicana, would be a promotion for him, and he looked forward to the opportunity of building a new company.

Although Ted had not worked outside the United States before, he felt confident that his managerial abilities would transfer "south of the border." He and his wife enjoyed vacationing in Cancun and they both liked Mexican food, so the idea of spending a few years building a new company in Mexico appealed to him. Ted's wife, Kim was not as excited

3

about the move, since she and their two small children would have to leave family and friends. Kim would also probably not be working in Mexico, as she had done in the United States.

Before the move, both Ted and Kim read travel books on Mexico and visited Guadalajara to select suitable housing. While Kim had reservations about the move, she felt that it would be a good opportunity for Ted and that she and the children would learn to adapt to their new surroundings. After all, she reasoned, they were only planning on living in Mexico for two years; just long enough for Ted to get the plant up and running and profitable. None of the Dorman's spoke Spanish fluently; however, Kim thought that she could get by, since she had taken three years of Spanish in high school.

She had heard that Guadalajara was home to a large expatriate community, and that she could isolate herself and the children from Mexican culture if she felt the need. Ted would be working with English speakers mostly, and many people at the plant could do translating for him. A number of SterMexicana managers had been to the United States and were familiar with its culture. Ted and Kim concluded that cultural adaptation would not be difficult, and no matter how hard the assignment, its short duration was manageable.

When the family arrived in Guadalajara, Manuel Angel Menendez Mata met them at the airport. Manuel would be Ted's Mexican counterpart, acting in the official capacity of assistant plant manager, and unofficially as a cultural mentor. Ted and Kim were surprised by the warmth and friendliness of Manuel and his wife Adriana, and they felt very welcomed by their new Mexican friends. Over the next few days Manuel and Adriana helped the new expatriates get settled in and familiar with their new home. Ted appreciated the personal attention Manuel was giving him and his family; however, Ted was anxious to begin discussing the needs of the new business. It sometimes seemed to Ted that Manuel didn't care to discuss the business or that he was not very excited about the new opportunity. Manuel seemed more interested in showing Ted and his family the city and discussing its history, politics, and culture.

The Formal Mexican

Once the Dorman family had settled in, Ted was able to turn his attention toward the business. He had many matters to attend to, including a review of the preliminary work Manuel had done in securing the facility, hiring a work force, and establishing an organizational structure. Manuel explained what he had done and how it would work well. He predicted that the new plant would be fully functional in less than two weeks. Ted was very impressed with Manuel's work and looked forward to the opening of the plant.

During their many conversations, Ted felt that Manuel was very friendly and polite, but that he was a bit too formal and not very relaxed. Manuel wore a suit and tie, even when Ted told him that a more casual form of dress would be appropriate. Ted stated that he had no intention of ever wearing a tie the whole time he would be in Mexico. Manuel sometimes referred to Ted as "Mr. Dorman," even though Ted had instructed him to call him by his first name. During their meetings with outside business associates, Ted noticed that Manuel was even more formal. Manuel, who had visited the United States many times and spoke English very well, understood that Americans were more relaxed when it came to such matters, but he was not happy when Ted began to call him "Manny." Manuel was also unhappy with Ted's refusal to recognize his title, "Licenciado" (licensed one), and that he sometimes referred to him as Senor Mata.

Although things seemed to be progressing toward the opening of the plant, Ted began to worry that Manuel's estimate of when the plant would be functional was too optimistic. Manuel insisted that everything was on schedule and that there would be no problems. It did, however, become obvious as the days went by that the plant was not going to be ready, as Manuel had promised. Ted felt that he had been misled by Manny and that he would have to explain to his superiors back in the U.S. why the plant was not going to open on schedule. Manuel finally admitted that some problems had developed with work permits, but he assured Ted that the plant would be operational in an additional week's time. The plant finally opened, five weeks past the scheduled date.

Gringo Style Management

This delay had caused tension between Manuel and Ted, and Ted felt that he could not trust Manuel. Manuel felt that Ted was too impatient, and that he was not sensitive enough to the problems sometimes found in conducting business in Mexico. Manuel complained to a friend that Ted was trying to do business in Mexico, "gringo style." He offered as an example the failed attempt Ted had made to establish a business relationship with a new supplier. Manuel had arranged for a business lunch between Ted, himself, and representatives from a well-respected metals supplier. Manuel explained how Ted offended the Mexican businessmen by attempting to get down to business quickly. The supplier's representatives felt that Ted was too concerned about business matters, especially price, and that he was rushing to close a deal. They were also offended when Manuel offered to take the visiting businessmen on a tour of the city and show them some important cultural sites and Ted refused to come along. Ted later told Manuel that he felt that the suppliers were not really serious about getting SterMexicana's business, and that if they wanted to do business with the company, they would have to send only one representative to his office with samples and a price list. Ted told Manuel that he would no longer spend hours discussing politics, sports, and history without any consideration given to the actual business deal.

The plant had been functioning for about six months without any serious problems when Ted received word from corporate headquarters that the plant needed to improve its efficiency. The quality of the product was considered acceptable, however, the American managers were disappointed with the productivity of the plant. Sterling's main incentive for investing in Mexico was the desire to reduce its labor costs and improve its overall operational efficiency. Ted worried that his career mobility was in serious jeopardy if he did not make major improvements. With this in mind, Ted began to look more carefully at Manuel's work.

From the beginning Ted had turned over to Manuel the day-to-day responsibility for running the plant, but he now felt that he would have to intervene and make some significant changes. After analyzing the situation Ted concluded that three major changes should be made. He proposed to Manuel that an incentive pay system be introduced, that a more participative approach to decision making be implemented, and that a number of workers be fired.

The productivity level of the plant was considered low by American standards, and Ted felt that there was simply no incentive for workers to do more than the minimum level of work. He proposed a pay-for-performance plan in which workers would essentially be paid on a piece-rate basis. The workers would also be given more responsibility for planning and organizing their work, and, in some cases, even planning their own schedules. Ted felt that a more flexible scheduling system would eliminate the excessive time off requested by many workers to handle family matters. Ted also created a list of the lowest-performing workers and instructed Manuel to fire all of them immediately. Since the unemployment rate was much higher in Mexico than in the United States, Ted reasoned that he would have no problem replacing the workers.

Ted Pushes Harder

Manuel was stunned by what he was hearing from Ted. Manuel was upset, first, that Ted had chosen to invade his areas of responsibility, and he was further upset by Ted's recommendations. Manuel felt that Ted was being too aggressive and insensitive in labor relations matters, and that his recommendations would not be successful in Mexico. He told Ted that there would be problems with these proposed changes; however, Ted did not seem to want to listen.

Although Manuel did not agree with the recommendations, he did as Ted had instructed and began by firing some of the employees Ted had targeted as low performers. He then implemented the pay-for-performance plan and attempted to explain how it would work. Most workers felt confused by the complex, flexible working-hours plan, which involved basic quotas, a two-tiered pay system, and a time borrowing option, which could be used for personal time off, such as doctor's appointments. Manuel simplified the plan so that workers could go home when they had met their quota, or they could continue to work for additional compensation at a slightly lower per-unit rate. Ted felt that workers would be willing to work longer hours even at a reduced rate if their total compensation would rise. After all, he reasoned, "Mexico is a dirt-poor country and people really need money." Finally, Manuel told the plant supervisors about the plan to empower factory workers and allow them some of the decision-making authority that the supervisors had exercised in the past.

Ted had high hopes that his recommendations for change would produce significant improvements at SterMexicana. He was aware that Mexican culture was different from his; however, he felt that business activities were for the most part universal and that efficiency was not a cultural issue. Ted felt that the proposed changes would result in an immediate improvement in overall operating efficiency.

Slowly, however, Ted began to realize that problems were developing with his recommendations. The first problem he confronted was notification that severance pay would have to be paid to the employees he had recently fired. Ted was unaware, and Manuel did not mention, that Mexican law does not operate the same way as U.S. law, in which workers are considered to be hired at will and subject to at-will termination. Ted was also surprised to learn that not all the employees he had targeted for termination had, in fact, been fired. After investigating the situation further, he discovered that five of the employees whom he had instructed to be fired were still working for the company. Ted was shocked to learn that the five employees were close relatives of Manuel. When confronted with this fact, Manuel just shrugged his shoulders and told Ted that he could not bring himself to fire them.

Although Ted was upset with Manuel's insubordination, he was far more concerned with the lack of any productivity gains at the plant. He was told that most workers did complete their tasks more quickly under the incentive plan; however, they elected to go home rather than work additional hours for more money. Ted was confused by this behavior so he asked some of the supervisors to explain it. They didn't provide satisfactory answers so Ted decided that he should conduct interviews with the employees themselves. Working through an interpreter, Ted asked workers about their jobs and what he could do to make them more productive. He was frustrated by the lack of responses he was getting from the employees. When Ted probed more deeply he discovered that the supervisors had not implemented the participative management practices he had ordered.

Faced with poor operating results during the first year of operation, Ted wondered if the decision to take the job in Mexico had been a mistake. To make matters worse, Ted's family was very unhappy about living in Mexico. Ted had been working long hours at the plant and had basically discounted the complaints he had heard from his wife and children. At this point he began to feel that perhaps they were right in their frequent criticisms of Mexican culture. With over a year left in his assignment in Mexico Ted felt frustrated and wondered what he should do next.

SOURCES

R. Malat, <u>Passport Mexico</u>. (1996). San Rafael, CA: World Trade Press.
R Sanyal. (2001). <u>International Management: A Strategic Perspective</u>. Upper Saddle River, NJ: Prentice Hall.
J. Scarborough. (2001). <u>The Origins of Cultural Differences and Their Impact on Management</u>. Westport, CT: Quorum.

This case was prepared by Charles A. Rarick and Inge Nickerson.

CASE 2

AU REVOIR, MRS. WILLIAMSON

ABSTRACT

Margaret Williamson, a British expatriate had been assigned to Paris as a marketing manager for a British-French joint venture called EUROi. While Margaret had been a successful manager in London, she did not continue that success in Paris and experienced many difficulties in her new assignment. Margaret was unable to work effectively with her French counterpart, Georges DuPont which was the result of personality differences, and differences in country and corporate culture. The inability to adjust to these challenges resulted in Margaret failing in her expatriate assignment and returning to London with an uncertain future in her company.

Margaret Williamson, age 50, has just returned to London from Paris, where she worked for the past six months as a marketing specialist for a British and French joint venture called EUROi. British computer manufacturer RoyalPC formed the joint venture with a French ISP called Internet du France (IDF). The two companies hope to capitalize on their particular strengths and grow a Pan-European Internet service. EUROi competes in Europe on the basis of price, and has positioned itself as an alternative ISP in an already crowded market. EUROi targets the 16 to 24 year-old market by offering programming that appeals to a more youthful market. The company also offers subscribers sizable discounts on Royal personal computers.

Margaret Williamson

Margaret began her career at Royal fifteen years ago as a secretary. As a recently divorced mother of two, Margaret entered the work force for the first time and displayed a strong work ethic. Although she did not attend college, Margaret is a very intelligent individual and a quick learner. These traits did not go unnoticed at Royal, and she was promoted out of the secretary pool and placed into the Marketing Department. Margaret advanced in the department, gaining a reputation for handling difficult assignments. With a strong devotion to her children and her work, she chose not to remarry. With her children now grown she became interested in an international assignment.

Her colleagues viewed Margaret as an effective manager. She was seen as fair to all, conscientious, a good decision maker, and very loyal to the company. Because of her abilities, she was selected to act as marketing liaison between her company and the French partner in the newly formed joint venture.

Mrs. Williamson, as she prefers to be called, is a refined British lady. She possesses excellent manners and prides herself on her personal composure. Her ability to remain calm and level-headed in tense situations would be challenged when she moved to Paris for her new assignment. Georges DuPont, age 35, is director of marketing for EUROi. DuPont, a graduate of the prestigious Ecole Nationale d' Administration, comes from an elite French family. Somewhat of a renegade, Georges refused to work in the family business after college. He instead, found employment in a number of computer-related businesses. DuPont became fascinated with the creative side of the computer and Internet business. He had been at IDF for four years, and was highly regarded as an effective manager and creative promoter. As marketing director of the joint venture, DuPont was given the responsibility of working with Williamson to find a way to increase revenue for EUROi. DuPont prides himself on his literary and artistic skills and enjoys engaging others in verbal debate.

Workplace Tensions

From the start of their working relationship, problems surfaced between Margaret and Georges. At first, small personal habits of the two seemed to cause friction. Margaret often remarked that Georges never smiled at her, and Georges called Margaret's personality as "interesting as a bottle of cheap California wine." Over the early weeks of the relationship, the situation deteriorated further. Margaret was convinced that Georges was an incompetent and lazy manager. She felt that Georges was too autocratic and did not delegate enough responsibility to lower levels in the organization. Margaret further complained to her superiors back in London that Georges frequently broke company policy, canceled meetings with little notice, took two-hour lunch breaks, and never admitted his mistakes. She felt that he did not respect her as an equal partner; in fact, she felt that he actually resented her help in promoting the joint venture.

To add more tension to the already strained relationship, Margaret learned that Georges (a married man) was having an affair with his secretary, Giselle. This fact came to light when Margaret found out that the two of them were going to a resort in the south of France for three weeks of vacation. Margaret was offended by Georges's lack of morality, which included his affair with Giselle as well as his advances to other women in the company.

Georges was equally unimpressed with Margaret. He felt that she was uneducated, insensitive, and too concerned with money and company regulations. Georges frequently joked to others about the way in which Margaret dressed. He felt that she had no taste in fashion, and that this alone made her abilities in the company suspect. Georges was unhappy that Margaret forced everyone to communicate with her in English. Although she spoke little French and Georges and most others spoke fluent English, he resented this, nevertheless. When Margaret requested that she be referred to as "Mrs. Williamson," Georges just rolled his eyes and muttered something in French that Margaret did not understand. He seldom used either her first or last name in conversations with her.

The workplace tensions continued for some time, with Georges and Margaret frequently disagreeing and complaining about each other. It was known throughout EUROi that the two did not get along, and their strained interactions were often the butt of jokes around the company. Georges tried to avoid Margaret as much as possible, which put her in the awkward position of having to go through Giselle to communicate with him. Margaret did not like to deal with Giselle because of her "illicit" behavior with her boss.

The Advertising Campaign

The situation finally came to a head when a creative team was to be assembled to design a large advertising campaign for EUROi. Margaret had already developed a plan to assemble the team and empower them with the responsibility of creating a more youth-oriented advertising theme. Margaret had identified five people whom she felt would be best suited for the project. Her plan was to allow these people to work independent of management in creating a new series of advertisements. Margaret felt that a more creative approach to promotion was needed, and she wanted this team to develop a breakthrough design for the promotional strategy.

When Margaret approached Georges with her idea, he refused to accept it. He told Margaret that he felt the current campaign was effective, but admitted that he could see a need for some improvement. Georges recommended that he solicit the advice of a few key people and that he create the new ad design. After all, he was the director of marketing for the new company. Margaret tried to explain to Georges why her plan was better, and that a similar approach had been successful with RoyalPC. Georges just stared at the ceiling, smoking his cigarette. Margaret wasn't even sure if he was listening to her.

London Calling

After a few weeks of attempting to convince Georges that her plan was better, Margaret decided that she needed help from London. She arranged for a video conference call to be held between London and Paris, in which she and some senior managers at Royal would discuss the issue further with Georges. Margaret sent an e-mail message to Georges, informing him of the conference but received no response. After two days, she asked Giselle if her boss knew of the proposed meeting and if he could attend. Giselle just smiled and responded that he could attend the meeting, if he desired to do so. Margaret sent a memo to Georges indicating the date and time of the conference call and emphasizing the importance of his presence at the meeting.

On the day of the meeting, Margaret searched for Georges. Even though the meeting wasn't for a few hours, she wanted to make sure he would attend, and she thought that perhaps she could even get him to change his mind before the call took place. Giselle told Margaret that he would be in the office soon and that she would remind him of the meeting.

As the 1:00 P.M. hour for the meeting approached, Margaret was frantic. She phoned Giselle and demanded to know where Georges was and when he would be in the conference room. Giselle responded that she didn't know where he was and that she really didn't care. When Giselle rudely hung up the phone, Margaret was convinced that Georges would not show up for the meeting. She decided, however, that she might be able to use this to her advantage.

The call from London came precisely at 1:00 PM, with just Margaret sitting in the Paris office. She explained to the people in London that

Georges was not present and that she had no idea why he was not there. She went on to tell the London managers that she was not surprised by Georges's behavior; he continually expressed contempt for her, and he had an apparent disregard for the welfare of EUROi. Margaret went on for over 30 minutes detailing Georges's shortcomings, when suddenly he entered the room with three other EUROi employees. Georges apologized for his tardiness but explained that he and the others had been across town working with marketing personnel from a very popular magazine targeted toward the 16 to 24 age group in Europe. Georges was very excited about what this "team" had accomplished, and he wanted the London managers to know the details.

The video call went on for another hour with the three EUROi employees explaining with charts and figures how the association with the youth magazine would be beneficial to the company. They proposed new creative advertising designs and an association with the popular magazine. The team appeared to have been well prepared for the meeting. Georges, who spoke with great confidence and enthusiasm, directed the entire presentation. From the questions asked by the London managers, it was clear that they felt Georges's plan was superior to the one proposed by Margaret. When the presentation was completed they thanked Georges and his team and quickly approved the plan.

At that point Margaret rose from her chair, red-faced and very angry. She appeared at first barely able to speak, but when she began, she angrily accused Georges of undermining her authority. Margaret called Georges a "sneaky bastard," and for the next five minutes vented her frustration at Georges, who sat quietly staring at the ceiling, smoking his cigarette. Finally the most senior London manager interrupted Margaret and politely asked if Georges and his team could leave the room for a moment. Georges got up and began to leave, but before he left he stopped, smiled at Margaret, and said, "au revoir, *Mrs.* Williamson."

SOURCES

Joseph, N. (1997). Passport France. Novato, CA: World Trade Press.
Scarborough, J. (1998). The Origins of Cultural Differences and Their Impact on Management. Westport, CT: Quorum.

This case was prepared by Charles A. Rarick.

CASE 3

POLSKA PIPE WORKS

Managing an IJV in the Transitional Economy of Poland

ABSTRACT

William Zukowski, an American expatriate of Polish ancestry was given the opportunity by his company, Stewer Technologies, to head a small joint venture in Poland. Zukowski experiences a number of difficulties in attempting to institute American management practices such as pay-for-performance, quality management, participative management, and lean manufacturing. The case also addresses a number of cross-cultural management issues.

Introduction

With the fall of communism in the former Soviet Union and its Eastern European neighbors in the early 1990's market opportunities opened for Western companies which had not previously been available. The American pipe manufacturer, Stewer Technologies had previously exported in small quantities high-density polyethylene pipes to Poland. These pipes were used in Poland's major cities for sewer and drainage. With the end of communism and the dawn of a free market economy in Poland, Stewer Technologies took steps to expand its market opportunities in Poland and other Central and Eastern European countries. With the liberalization of foreign joint venture law and its existing business associations, Stewer was able to find a Polish partner to begin the manufacture of polyethylene pipes in the Polish city of Krakow.

The market for sewer and drainage pipes was rather limited during the previous fifteen years due to the lack of resources of the Polish government. Recently, the federal government of Poland began an ambitious program of infrastructure improvement in an effort to bring Poland's major cities up to the standards of Western Europe. Very little high-density polyethylene sewer pipe was manufactured domestically, and the Polish pipe that was produced domestically was considered to be of inferior quality. Most polyethylene pipe used in Poland was imported from the United States and Western Europe. Stewer saw this situation to be an excellent opportunity to produce quality pipe in Poland with lower labor and transportation costs, and the possibility of exporting to neighboring countries such as the Czech Republic, Slovakia, Belarus, Lithuania, and Hungary.

Poland

With a population of 38 million, Poland is the largest country in Eastern Europe. Poland is a very homogeneous country with ninety eight percent of its population being Polish. Poles are a Slavic people, proud of their heritage and ability to endure the ravages of many invaders and two world wars. Poland had been under the control of the former Soviet Union since the end of World War II, however, the Polish people did not embrace Soviet ideals, and in the late 1970s with a Polish Pope providing encouragement, the Polish people began a campaign for freedom. In the early 1980s Poland's labor movement flexed its muscles and gained concession from the government. During the decade political tensions ran high with the Polish labor movement, Solidarity making some gains and receiving some setbacks. By the end of the decade free elections were held and Solidarity leader Lech Walesa gained the presidency of the nation. Poland's post-communist government began an ambitious movement towards free market reform. Privatization of state-owned industry began, and laws were enacted to improve the business climate of the country. The Foreign Investment Act of 1991 encouraged foreign investment, and in most cases allowed up to 100 percent foreign ownership of businesses. Certain restrictions on foreign direct investment remain, however, including restrictions on investment in steel, mining, energy, banking, telecommunications, and broadcasting. Poland has been very successful in attracting foreign investment, with FDI in excess of $8 billion in 1999 and $12 billion in 2000. While the 1991 Act encourages FDI, foreign owned firms are placed at a competitive disadvantage in bidding on government contracts. If the foreign firm establishes a joint venture with a Polish company, however, the company can qualify as a domestic company and avoid the restrictions. This aspect of the law has made international joint ventures popular in Poland.

Stewer Technologies

In 1958 Fred Stewer started a small company to supply water and sewer pipes to the city of Chicago. The company grew over the years and in the 1980s the company began to receive orders for its products from abroad. International sales were not considered important to the company until the middle of the 1990s when this segment began to increase significantly and domestic sales began to drop. The company realized that the international market was not only more lucrative in most cases, but also that it may be necessary to cultivate it in order for the company to survive. Stewer established an international division in 1995 and began to promote its products through international trade shows and with the help of federal government agencies.

Stewer Technologies had been exporting small quantities of polyethylene pipe to Poland since 1989; however, the sales figures were too low for much attention to be paid to the country. All that changed in 1998 when the company was approached by a Polish contractor who proposed that a joint venture be established to supply the Polish government with sewer and water pipes for its large-scale infrastructure renewal program. The idea seemed like a good one in that Polish labor costs were quite low compared to the United States, and the company could avoid transportation costs and tariffs. The potential for export to other Central and Eastern European countries also made the proposal appealing.

Polska Pipe Works and William Zukowski

The city of Krakow was chosen from three competing cities in Poland and construction of the plant began in 1999 and was completed in 2000. The joint venture was named Polska Pipe Works. It was decided that an American manager from Stewer Technologies would be chosen as plant manager or Managing Director, but that almost all other employees would be Polish. With a relatively high unemployment rate in Poland it was easy to find workers for the plant. The Polish partner recruited and selected the Polish workforce. The Polish partner also established the organizational structure, created job descriptions, and helped determine compensation and benefits. Most Poles were very happy to be able to work for an American company in that they perceived that the American company would be able to provide job security and higher wages. The wages which were low by American standards were much higher than that offered by similar domestic companies in Poland. American workers at Stewer Technologies were not unionized and the company hoped to keep its Polish operation non-union as well. It was believed that if compensation was set significantly above the standard domestic rate employees would see no advantage to unionization. To supplement the Polish workforce, a temporary team of experienced American workers was selected to work in Krakow in order to help train the Polish workers.

William Zukowski, a 19-year veteran of Stewer Technologies was selected to head the Polish operation. Trained in engineering and management, Zukowski had held a number of positions in the company, but this position would be his first opportunity to head an entire facility. Zukowski was considered to be a good candidate for the position in that he had an excellent track record at Stewer, and that he had some understanding of Polish culture. Zukowski's grandparents had immigrated to Chicago from Poland and he maintained ties with the Polish community of Chicago. Although not fluent in Polish, he did speak some of the language and had visited the country while on vacation in 1996. Zukowski eagerly accepted the assignment for two reasons. Most importantly, he felt that the position offered an excellent opportunity for advancement, and he did have an emotional attachment to the Polish people and felt that it would be important to teach them American methods of management. Zukowski moved to Poland with his wife Sandy and their three children, Stefan, age 14, Elizabeth, age 12, and John, age 8. The family was excited, yet somewhat anxious about the move. It was never very clear how long the family would be living in Poland.

Early Difficulties

After the Zukowski family arrived and settled in Krakow, William began to assume his duties at Polska. William felt that employee development was a top priority and that he should spend much of his time in the supervision of employee training programs. Zukowski also decided that he would train some key managers himself. His initial contacts with Polska employees seemed to indicate to him that the employees were very receptive to learning Western business practices.

One of the first areas in which Zukowski sought to train workers was in the area of quality management. Zukowski had instructed managers at Stewer in TQM, and he lead a special projects team, which helped the company, achieve ISO 9000 certification. He had attended one of the seminars conducted by the late quality guru Edwards Deming and was fascinated by his approach to management. Zukowski hoped to quickly implement a quality management program and gain ISO 9000 certification for Polska.

At first it appeared that the managers who had been selected for the training were motivated to learn. Over time, however, it seemed that the managers kept asking questions unrelated to the training. More and more the managers were asking about compensation and benefits and fewer and fewer questions about the training material. For example, it became very clear that the Polish managers had determined that the American workers who came to Krakow on temporary assignment were being paid much more. The Polish managers were also comparing company benefits and found out that the Americans were receiving more benefits than the Poles. Zukowski tried to answer the questions and respond to the objections as quickly as possible and then to resume his training efforts. Not everyone was satisfied with his answers.

One of the more vocal Polish managers, Michal Gorzko was often difficult to silence during the training sessions. He often complained that the American company showed preferential treatment to the Americans. He also expressed his dissatisfaction with the fact that many of the Americans were younger than most of the Polish managers and that they treated the Polish managers as if "they were their children." Gorzko felt that the older Americans were skilled and experienced workers but that they should not be perceived as being more valuable to the company. Gorzko, a graduate of Warsaw University also seemed to resent the fact that people without a college education would be making more money. Zukowski tried to explain how the Americans were only going to be in Poland temporarily and that they had to be compensated by American cost-of-living standards. Over time it became clear that Gorzko was acting as a spokesperson for the entire group of Polish managers. After this initial training effort Zukowski decided that he should delegate the training function to others.

There were also personal difficulties in the early days for William Zukowski. His family was not adjusting well to their new environment. At first the experience seemed exciting for Sandy. Living in a foreign country was always something she had wanted to do and she felt that the experience would be good for the children. Although the children were unhappy from the start, with their mother's encouragement and understanding, she was able to make the experience less traumatic. The children missed their friends back in Chicago and they were not happy with their new America style school. The children also missed the comforts and recreational activities they had become accustomed to back in the United States. William was very busy at work and was seldom available even on weekends to be with the family. At first Sandy accepted the hardships, but over time she began increasingly to complain about her life in Poland including the lack of friendship, the poor telephone service and roads, and the difficulty of communicating with people who did not speak English. Life was much harder in Poland than she had expected.

Proposed Changes

At work, having finally completed the quality training sessions, Jukowski moved on to other areas. He decided to change some of the operational policies which the Polish partner had established for the joint venture. In particular he wanted to reduce the level of bureaucracy, change compensation to a more performance-based system, and institute a participative, teamwork approach to management. Zukowski felt the present system created by Stewer's Polish partner was too much like old Eastern Bloc management.

With the help of a young Polish manager named Tomasz Fusinski, Zukowski began an assessment of the organizational structure of Polska. The two worked out a plan to reduce many administrative positions and save the joint venture considerably on salary expense. However, Fusinski, feeling uneasy about the changes did speak up, providing a prophetic warning. "Mister Director, enjoyment in the summer can come at the expense of comfort in the winter." Zukowski wasn't quite sure what the young manager was trying to tell him and he dismissed the advice as some unimportant old Polish lure. The changes were implemented as directed by Zukowski with considerable unhappiness among the entire workforce. The changes meant that not only would positions be eliminated among the office staff, but that production positions would also be cut as well. Outsourcing of some supplies and a reduction in many support positions would make the manufacturing process leaner, and more productive. Ultimately this would allow for more compensation for the remaining employees. Zukowski felt that some employees would resent the layoffs but that most would find the thought of making more money "music to their ears."

Zukowski felt that the workers of Polska were either not motivated, or that they simply didn't understand modern management practices.

He felt that an improved system of financial rewards would give them an incentive to work harder. Zukowski was concerned by the fact that workers routinely left for home at around 4PM, even if the plant had an urgent need for production. Consistent with company policy in Chicago, and previously agreed upon between the partners, all employees at Polska were paid a salary. There were no hourly employees in either company. Although this compensation system seemed to work in the United States, Zukowski wondered if it was appropriate in Poland, given the recent experience with the communist system. He worried that such a plan may be abused by the Polish workers. In response he met with some of the higher-level Polish managers and ask for their advice. The managers who were always very formal, and respectful, failed to give him much guidance. Zukowski, therefore, created a new compensation plan himself and gained its approval from Chicago. The new plan was called "ZlotyShare" using the name of the Polish currency the zloty, and indicating that it was a form of the American practice of gainsharing. The new plan was complex but basically meant that compensation would be tied to worker productivity and cost reductions.

Immediately upon announcement of the new compensation program the Polish employees rebelled, including most of Polska's managers. Although Zukowski explained that the new program was an attempt to allow workers to make more money, few accepted the idea. Zukowski could not understand why the workers would not want the opportunity to earn additional money and all his attempts to explain the program seemed to fall on deaf ears. It occurred to him the reason that he was receiving such resistance to his change effort was that it was too autocratic, and so he began to develop a more participative approach to decision making. Zukowski created a series of committees and appointed several high level Polish managers to head those committees. The purpose of the committees was to force authority down to lower levels of the organizational structure. Because of his past difficulties with Michal Gorzko, Zukowski did not appoint him to any of the committees. Although it appeared that the Polish managers liked the idea of the committees, Zukowski was disappointed in their progress. It appeared that they were only recommending superficial changes, and that they were mainly concerned with holding on to, or increasing, their own power. Frustrated with their success Zukowski disbanded the committees.

After consulting some friends back in Chicago and discussing the ideas with his now trusted Polish advisor Tomasz Fusinski, Zukowski announced a new organizational structure, once again. Productivity and quality had been steadily dropping since the introduction of the ZlotyShare plan and the downsizing effort. Zukowski needed something to work, and work quickly. He announced that young Fusinski was being promoted to the position of Assistant Director and Manager of Special Teams. Fusinski would be supervising the introduction of a production team structure, similar to the one used by Stewer in the United States. It was announced that team leaders would be selected based on interviews by Zukowski and Fusinski, and that the team leaders would receive sizable increases in salary. The positions would be open to all production employees. Present managers could apply, but they would not be assured a team leader position.

Triad of Despair

William Zukowski was aware of the anxiety which his changes had produced for the employees of Polska. He did not want to make their work environment difficult, however, he was convinced that some pain was necessary in order to change the Polish mindset which had developed over the many years of Soviet domination. He was prepared to endure some pain himself, however, he was not prepared for the events which would occur on the Monday morning following the week he proposed his latest changes.

After a stressful weekend with the family it was decided that Sandy and the children would return to the United States by Christmas, and that William would stay in Krakow for the duration of his assignment. It was a difficult decision, but all family members agreed that it would be best. William would fly home every month to visit and Sandy and the children would resume their life as usual back in Chicago.

On the way to work that morning William began to lament his decision to accept the Polish assignment. He was still confident in his ability to make improvements in the operation and to advance his career, however, he did not like the toll it was taking on his family. He also lamented the missed opportunities he had planned to tour Poland with his family and enjoy its rich history. As he continued to work he vowed that he would quickly improve the operating results of Polska and then ask to be returned to Chicago.

When Zukowski arrived at the office he was met with very disturbing information. He first noticed that a letter of resignation was on his desk from Tomasz. The letter was very brief and apologetic and offered no reason for the resignation. Zukowski was very surprised and personally hurt by the sudden departure of his trusted young advisor. Not having much time to absorb the resignation, Zukowski was hit again with bad news. His assistant informed him that many of the workers had refused to come to work today and that Michal Gorzko was leading a drive to unionize all plant personnel. Thinking of his family, the loss of his Polish advisor, and the threat of unionization, Zukowski looked out the window of his office and realized that the coming Polish winter may in fact be very uncomfortable.

SOURCES

Cullen, J. (2002). Multinational Management: A Strategic Approach. Cincinnati: South- Western.

Crane, R. (2000). European Business Cultures. Harlow, England: Financial Times/ Prentice Hall.

Davies, N. (2001) Heart of Europe: A Short History of Poland. Oxford: Oxford University Press.

Heale, J. (1999). Cultures of the World: Poland. New York: Marshall Cavendish.

Johnson, S. (1995). *Starting Over: Poland after Communism*. Harvard Business Review, March-April.

Kissel, N. (2000). Passport Poland. Novato, CA: World Trade Press.

Mead, R. (1998). International Management. Oxford: Blackwell Publishing.

O'Driscoll, G., Holmes, K. and M. Kirkpatrick. (2001). Index of Economic Freedom. Washington: Hertage Foundation and New York: Wall Street Journal.

Sanyal, R. (2001). International Management. Upper Saddle, NJ: Prentice Hall.

WWW.Countrywatch.Com

WWW.Poland.Pl

This case was prepared by Charles A. Rarick and Gregory Winter and previously published in the Proceedings of the 6th International Conference on Global Business and Economic Development, November, 2001.

CASE 4

DEAD SEA SALT PROCESSING:
A Bitter Mix of Cultures

ABSTRACT

The Dead Sea Salt Works, located in the West Bank, is a major processor and exporter of salt. The case examines cultural difficulties involving employees from Israel, Russia, Palestine, and the United States. Employees from each of these countries are selected to form a new export team that eventually becomes very unsuccessful. The case explores multi-cultural management and conflict resolution issues.

Ezra Maser is the managing director of The Dead Sea Salt Works, located in Hebron, in the West Bank. The Dead Sea Salt Works is Israel's largest processor of salt, and the company employs 630 employees from a number of countries. The company, which is publicly traded on the Tel-Aviv Stock Exchange, processes seawater into salt for household and industrial uses. The Dead Sea Salt Works also has begun to develop a business of extracting other minerals from the area including magnesium and bromine. The company has been highly successful in its 12-year existence using solar evaporation plants to extract salt from the Dead Sea. Most of the company's salt product is exported to Europe, and some parts of the Middle East.

Hebron, the location of the company's headquarters is an ancient city, and one of great importance to Christians, Muslims, and Jews in that it is believed that Abraham is buried there in the Cave of Machpelah. Abraham is an important figure to all three religions and Hebron has often been the site of bitter conflicts between Arabs and Jews. Ezra has seen his share of conflict in the six years he has lived in Hebron but he is somewhat surprised by the recent level of conflict he has witnessed among some of his employees.

The State of Israel

The State of Israel has within its borders land that is considered sacred to three religions: Judaism, Christianity, and Islam. Israelis call Jerusalem the capital, however, most nations do not recognize Jerusalem as Israel's capital and locate their embassies in Tel-Aviv. Israel is a parliamentary democracy founded in 1948 by a United Nations agreement that sought to provide a state for the Jewish Diaspora. Palestine was divided into Jewish and Arab territories, with Jerusalem being controlled by U.N. forces due to its extreme importance to both Arabs and Jews.

Arabs have been living in Palestine for hundreds of years. Jews had previously lived in Palestine (Israel) but were driven out by the Romans. Conquered by the Ottoman Empire, control of Palestine was assumed by the British after World War I. The British supported a Jewish state in Palestine, but also promised the Palestinians that they too would have a state of their own. In 1948 the United Nations divided Palestine into Jewish and Arab sectors, and Palestinians were forced to leave the Jewish territory. The 1967 War or "Six Day War" expanded Israel's control into the occupied territories, including the West Bank and the Gaza Strip. The Palestinians feel that the Israelis have stolen their land, and the Jews feel that this land was promised to them by God. Tension and violence has existed between the Israelis and Palestinians since the first wave of Jewish immigrants started arriving in Palestine after World War II. The Palestinians greatly resent the concept of a Jewish state in Palestine.

The Export Team

The Dead Sea Salt Works depends on exports. In order to sustain and grow the business, the company must continue to develop new export markets. Although export sales have been increasing, it was felt that a major push should be undertaken in order to ensure a stable income stream for the company. The Dead Sea Salt Works wanted to further develop its business in the export of other minerals as well, so Ezra Masser decided to assemble a team of specialists in order to find ways of improving export sales. He selected five employees from different functional areas of the company to work together for six months to develop a plan and to begin implementation of that plan in hopes of increasing export sales for the company.

Team Members

Benjamin Levy – Team Manager
Graduated from Tel Aviv University with a degree in economics.
Born in Israel
Employed as a manager for Dead Sea Works for eight years.
Age 31, Married with two children

Orli Avigad – Team Assistant Manager
Graduated from Bar-Llan University with a degree in accounting.
Served in Israeli military as an officer.
Employed as an accountant at Dead Sea Works for two years.
Age 27, Single

Dmitry Cherviakov – Team Scientist
Graduated from the Moscow Institute of Physics and Technology with a doctorate in geology.
Russian Jew who immigrated to Israel after the fall of the Soviet Union.
Employed as a geologist for Dead Sea Works for four years.
Age 36, Single

Azmi Shadid – Production Specialist
Graduated from Al-Quds University with masters degree in applied technology.
Palestinian who was born in Jerusalem.
Employed as a production specialist at Dead Sea

Works for six months.
Age 23, Married with one child.

Victoria Snowhill – Marketing Specialist
Graduated from the University of Michigan with a degree in marketing.
American expatriate working in Israel as a freelance export consultant.
Previous experience in United States as manager of exports for large U.S. coal company.
Age 32, Divorced with no children.

The export team was selected based on their special knowledge and technical skills. Benjamin was selected to lead the team because he was regarded as an effective manager, and he had proven himself in difficult tasks. Benjamin was held in high esteem by top management and it was widely rumored that he was on the fast track to move into the higher management ranks.

At first the team seemed to function fairly well. Benjamin relied heavily on Orli for coordination of tasks and to assign responsibilities. Most of the team members respected Orli, however, there were some early difficulties with Dmitry and Azmi. Both seemed to attempt to by pass Orli on occasion and go directly to Benjamin. When Benjamin instructed them to work with Orli they generally agreed and the issue was settled. Victoria and Orli worked together well and Orli relied on Victoria's expertise in export management. While some tensions also existed between Dmitry and Victoria, the team seemed to function well during the first month. The first month was spent preparing marketing opportunities for the current and future products that Dead Sea Works hoped to develop. Orli developed a list of 15 new markets that looked promising, and Dmitry worked on the product mix that seemed most appropriate to each export market. Azmi investigated the feasibility of Dead Sea Works supplying the product, and Victoria investigated the technical requirements of importing to each market. Benjamin reported to Ezra that the team was making good progress.

Early Problems

Dmitry Cherviakov was admitted to Israel under its policy of granting citizenship to all Jews, regardless of where they were born. After the fall of communism in the former Soviet Union it became difficult for many scientists to earn a living. Although not especially religious, Dmitry decided to immigrate to Israel as he saw the possibility of earning a good living working in a scientific field. When no suitable positions were offered to him in this area, he reluctantly decided to accept the position with Dead Sea Salt Works. Although the position was not regarded as prestigious, he was able to earn significantly more money than he could make in Russia.

While Dmitry did what was considered high-quality work, he did not seem to possess the work ethic that was expected at Dead Sea Salt Works. He was frequently late for work and often left early. Orli suspected that Dmitry had a drinking problem; however, she had no evidence to support her suspicions. When she confronted him on his tardiness and early departures he always came up with what appeared to be reasonable excuses. Nevertheless, Orli had concerns that Dmitry felt the position was below him and that he was simply not interested in such a position. She was also concerned with his insistence that people around him call him Dr. Cherviakov, and his condensing attitude towards others, especially Arab employees of the company. His initial interactions with Azmi were good, but they did not work together closely and Azmi keep his distance from Dmitry.

One team member who first complained about Dmitry was Victoria. While the two seemed to get along reasonably well in the first month of the project, things got much worse as time passed. While Victoria respected Dmitry's technical skills, she was often put off by his brass attitude and frequent sexual remarks. It was clear to Victoria that Dmitry had a romantic interest in her, but this interest was not mutual. Dmitry made rather direct advances towards her, and Victoria complained to Benjamin about this behavior, however, it appeared to have no effect. Benjamin told her that in order to cope with Israeli culture she would have to become a "sabra." A sabra is a cactus fruit that grows in Israel with a tough skin on the outside and a sweet taste inside. This advice did not satisfy Victoria, however, she decided that she would try to adapt. Victoria was, nevertheless, certain that such behavior would constitute sexual harassment in the United States. In addition to her concerns that Benjamin did not seem to take this matter seriously, Victoria was also offended by some of the terms of endearment he used when speaking to her.

Increasing Tensions

While the difficulties between Victoria and Dmitry were causing some problems with the team's functioning, the difficulties, which later developed between Azmi and Dmitry, were even more serious. Azmi had a general dislike of Dmitry, but for the most part he kept his thoughts to himself. On occasion he would express his feelings to Victoria, and the two would each take some comfort in knowing that they were not alone in their dislike of Dmitry. While Azmi kept his distance from Dmitry as much as possible and did not openly express his dissatisfaction with him, Dmitry could often be heard expressing his feelings about Azmi. Dmitry referred to Azmi as "Little Arafat" and accused him of being the leader of a terrorist organization. It was clear from his conversations with others that Dmitry did not like the Palestinians and that he did not care if anyone disagreed with him. Dmitry spent much time discussing politics in the office halls and offices and he could frequently be seen chatting with Benjamin.

The tension that existed between Dmitry and Azmi was starting to put a strain on the team effort of the group. Initially Orli blamed Dmitry for the tension, expressing to Benjamin her feelings that Dmitry was also unmotivated and undisciplined. He seldom reported to work on time and seldom worked beyond the minimum time required for his employment. Orli was also concerned about the effect this personal conflict between Azmi and Dmity was having on Victoria, who often expressed her dissatisfaction over Dmitry's "prejudicial and unfeeling nature." Dmitry and Benjamin, however, seemed to get along well, and Benjamin seemed rather uninterested in the problems Orli was having with him. Benjamin told her to respect Dmitry's abilities and gradually increase her expectations with regards to his performance. Benjamin promised that he would talk to Dmitry about his attitude, but he also told Orli that Azmi could handle the discrimination he was experiencing, and that it was impossible for him to avoid it.

Trip to the Big Orange

After three months of study and prospecting, the team was ready to make its first sales presentation on a trip to Tel Aviv. Victoria, Azmi, and Dmitry traveled to meet potential customers from Egypt and Germany. Dmitry was excited about the trip to the "Big Orange" and he told Victoria that such a trip would make a "new woman or just a woman out of her." Dmitry's enthusiasm was not shared by either Victoria or Azmi. Victoria's only concern was how the three-team members would make the two important sales presentations. Azmi was concerned about any travel in the country, and did not like to be away from his family overnight. He did realize the importance of the trip and was willing to accompany the other team members to Tel Aviv.

The first day of the trip was intended for travel and preparation. The two important potential customers would meet the team during the following two days to discuss proposals for extended business contracts. Arriving in Tel Aviv by early afternoon, the three checked into their hotel and made plans to meet in an hour to discuss the proposals and their strategy for the meetings. The team felt that because Victoria spoke some German and Azmi was Palestinian, that they would have an advantage in the meetings. After about an hour of discussing their strategy, Dmitry suggested to Victoria that the two of them go to the beach for a game of beach tennis. Azmi objected but Dmitry told him to "go down to the bar and have a few drinks and if you become a real person then you can join us at the beach." Azmi stormed out of the room and Victoria went with Dmitry to the beach. On the way to the beach Victoria told Dmitry that he was being difficult and that he should apologize to Azmi. Victoria also told Dmitry that it was important that the three-team members work together to plan the sales presentations. She insisted that they return from the beach in short order to get back to work.

After enjoying a fun filled day together Victoria and Dmitry seemed to be relating to each other better. Although Victoria still felt that Dmitry was chauvinistic, she did feel that he was intelligent and fun to be with. The first day in Tel Aviv ended, however, on a sad note as news of a suicide bombing in Hebron reached the team members. When Victoria and Dmitry found Azmi at the hotel he appeared very anxious and informed them that he would be returning home that evening. Victoria explained to Azmi that she understood his concerns, however, she felt that it was necessary that he be present at the meetings in order to help sell the company's products to the potential new customers. She explained how important it would be for him to be present, especially during the meeting with the Egyptian buyer. Azmi apologized but left for Hebron that evening.

During the next two days Victoria and Dmitry met with representatives of the German and Egyptian companies and attempted to convince them of the benefits of buying from the Dead Sea Works. They felt that the sales presentations went well, however, Victoria lamented the loss of Azmi. One of the German representatives did express concern over the ability of the company to supply salt and magnesium in a consistent fashion with the increasing activities of the intifada or civilian uprising of the Palestinian people. Victoria and Dmitry tried to reassure him that the company could continue to be a reliable supplier. After the meetings Victoria and Dmitry returned to Hebron optimistic that at least one of the potential buyers would sign a contract with the company. It was becoming increasing important that the team begin to show results and increase the export ability of the company.

When Dmitry and Victoria returned to work the following day they found the office in a somber mood. Tensions were a bit high and Orli was in an especially bad mood. Victoria attempted to talk to her, but Orli only complained about Azmi. Victoria defended Azmi saying that he was concerned about his family and that he was a hard worker. Orli appeared to doubt what Victoria was saying. Benjamin who barged into Orli's office to announce that he had received word that neither of the two buyers would be signing a contract with the company interrupted the conversation. Benjamin blamed Azmi for the loss of at least one of the sales, and when Victoria attempted to come to his defense, Benjamin rudely told her that she was wrong about Azmi being a good worker. He told her that if that were true Azmi would have stayed and helped make the sale. Benjamin was also critical of Dmitry who had not yet shown up for work. Victoria tried to defend Dmitry, only to be criticized by Benjamin for not appreciating the importance of the two lost sales.

Orli decided to call a meeting to discuss the reasons for the contract losses, and to decide a course of action. She scheduled a meeting later in the day, feeling confident that Dmitry would be in the office by then. She had no idea if Azmi was at work and really didn't seem to care. Victoria returned to her office to review some data until the meeting. After a few minutes Dmitry came into her office and gave her a big hug and a kiss on the check. Victoria was stunned by Dmitry's actions, however, she didn't mind, as she had grown fonder of him since the trip to Tel Aviv. It was at that moment that Azmi also arrived in her office, and upon seeing the two of them he immediately left the office. Victoria ran after Azmi to inquire about his family. Azmi seemed very agitated and only stated that his wife and son were fine. He did not ask about the sales meetings in Tel Aviv and left Victoria after being informed of the team meeting later in the day.

The Six-Minute War

When Victoria, Dmitry, and Azmi met in Orli's office later in the day to discuss the Tel Aviv meetings the conversation immediately turned to Azmi's absence. Once again Azmi answered the question as to the reason for his absence as a concern for the safety of his family. At that moment Dmitry stood up and accused Azmi of being a terrorist. He told Orli that he was certain that Azmi was a member of Hamas and that he was involved in terrorist activity in the city. Azmi appeared very angry but he remained silent as Dmitry continued to make accusations against him. Orli sat quietly and did not appear upset, however, Victoria could not believe Dmitry's action. She stood up and told Dmitry that he had no proof and that it was very unkind and irresponsible for him to make such charges against a fellow team member. Orli still remained quiet and did not ask Dmitry to stop even after she was asked by Victoria. Azmi then rose, and Victoria thought that he was going to defend himself against the accusations, but he instead turned on Victoria and accused her being "nothing but an American whore." Victoria, shocked by what she was hearing immediately left the room. Dmitry smiled at Orli and followed Victoria out of the office. Azmi stormed out of the office saying something in Arabic. The meeting had only lasted a few minutes but it became clear to Orli that she had a serious problem to solve. She decided that it was time for Benjamin to intervene and she proceeded to his office for a meeting. She met him in the hall and explained what had happened. Benjamin told her that this group of workers could no longer function as a team and that he was going to terminate some of the members. He told her that he would have to seek her advice on whom to fire and that Ezra would have to be informed.

Decisions

The following day all team members reported to work, except Azmi. Victoria and Dmitry were summoned into Orli's office and from the expression on her face, it was clear that she was very unhappy. Orli told them that it was certain that the team could not function as an effective working group and that it had been decided that Azmi and Victoria would no longer be employed by the Dead Sea Salt Works. Victoria could not believe what she was hearing, and was so stunned by the news that she did not question the decision. Shocked by the decision she sought comfort in Dmitry who would only say that it was "too bad that Little Arafat had brought his terror into your life." He wished her good luck and left for lunch. Victoria wondered what she should do, and then decided that she should request a meeting with Mr. Maser.

Ezra Maser granted Victoria her request for a meeting and sat quietly as Victoria recounted all the difficulties the team had experienced in its short existence. Ezra seemed very concerned as he listened to Victoria tell the details of the story, often with tears in her eyes. The meeting was interrupted by Benjamin who entered the office to inform Ezra that he had just heard that Azmi's uncle had been killed by an Israeli soldier on the evening of the suicide bombing. Benjamin asked that some form of condolence be sent to Azmi. As Ezra heard the news from Benjamin, and as he reflected on the information Victoria was providing wondered how things had gone so badly and what he should now do.

Charles Rarick and Arifin Angriawan

SOURCES

Autonomous. (1999). *Israel's Culture Wars.* The Economist. April 24.

Bernards, N. (1990). The Palestinian Conflict. San Diego: Greenhaven Press.

Green, J. (2001). Nations of the World: Israel. New York: Raintree Steck-Vaughn Publishers.

Keyser, J. (2001). *Israeli Arabs Seeking Equal Rights Find Themselves at Crossroads After Attack on Jews.* Worldstream, November 3.

Lowenstein, S. (2000). The Jewish Cultural Tapestry. New York: Oxford Press.

Rosenthal, D. (1997). Passport Israel. San Rafael, CA: World Trade Press.

Rosenzweig, P. (1994). *National Culture and Management.* Harvard Business Review, March-April.

Ross, S. (1996). Causes and Consequences of the Arab-Israeli Conflict. Austin, TX: Raintree Steck-Vaughn Publishers.

Silverman, M. (1998). Israel: The Founding of a Modern Nation. New York: Dial Books.

Smith, D. (1999). Israel: The Culture. New York: Crabtree Publishing.

This case was prepared by Charles A. Rarick.

CASE 5

DANCING WITH AN ELEPHANT

Cultural Missteps in Managing a Thai Expatriate

ABSTRACT

Marianne Whitaker is very concerned about the success of one of her new account representatives, Pongpol Chatusipitak, a Thai national who has worked for her at Premuris Investments for only six months. Pongpol does not appear to Marianne to be very motivated and some of his behavior seems odd to her. A decision must be reached concerning his future with the company.

It was a typically beautiful day in Southern California as Marianne Whitaker peered out her office window at Premuris Investments to the streets below. Marianne was not able to enjoy the scenery, as she was very concerned about the performance of one of her financial services advisors, Pongpol Chatusipitak. Pongpol had been hired six months ago to help generate increased business from the large Thai business community of Southern California. Pongpol had not generated much business in the first few months, but recently his performance had improved. Marianne was also concerned about some of his personal and work behaviors. Marianne felt that she would like to fire Polpong, however, this choice may not be an option. She wondered out loud where she had gone wrong and if anything could be done to improve the situation.

Pongpol Chatusipitak

Pongpol Chatusipitak, or "Moo" as he liked to be called, was from Chaing Mai in northern Thailand. Pongpol graduated from Chulalongkorn University in Thailand with a degree in economics. After working for a Thai bank for three years he enrolled in the graduate program at the

University of Southern California to study finance. Upon completion of an M.B.A. degree from USC, Pongpol was hired by Premuris as a financial services advisor.

Marianne Whitaker remembers how she was struck by the warm and easygoing nature of Pongpol. He seemed to have a perpetual smile and appeared very conscientious. Pongpol did not have an outstanding academic record at USC, however, Marianne had discounted the importance of grades and was more concerned with what she considered to be a strong work ethic in Asian people. The fact that Pongpol had an M.B.A. from a respected school, and spoke fluent Thai, made him a good candidate for the position. Marianne felt that Pongpol would be able to make contacts with the Thai business community and help generate significant revenue from this group of successful entrepreneurs. Premuris had determined that due to the competitive nature of the financial services industry and the firm's relatively small size, it was necessary for the company to branch out into more select niche markets. It was decided to begin with the Thai business community of Southern California.

Thailand

Thailand, a country whose name means "free land" was never colonized by a foreign power. It is a very homogeneous country with approximately 84% of its citizens being Thai and 14% Chinese. Most Thai's are Theravada Buddhists. Thailand is a constitutional monarchy and its people are considered nationalistic. The Thai flag consists of five horizontal stripes with the colors red, white, and blue. Red represents the nation, white represents Buddhism, and blue represents the monarchy. All three elements are important to most Thai's. Thailand is sometimes referred to as the sixth "Asian Tiger," with the other five being Japan, Korea, Hong Kong, Singapore, and Taiwan. Thailand experienced rapid economic growth during the 1980s and strengthened its industrial base. Overbuilding and real estate speculation lead to a rapid devaluation of Thailand's currency, the bath, in 1997. The devaluation and its subsequent financial turmoil put the Thai economy into a tailspin, and caused economic difficulties in neighboring countries.

Hired by Premuris

It was in 1997 that Pongpol decided to leave Thailand and head for the United States to pursue a graduate degree. He had chosen USC because several friends had chosen to attend the school, and because of its location.

While attending graduate school Pongpol worked as a waiter in a local Thai restaurant. The restaurant provided a place for him to live, and some badly needed income. While working in the restaurant, Pongpol met Stacy, a young American woman and the two became close friends. Because of his relationship with Stacy and the better employment opportunities in the United States, Pongpol decided not to return to Thailand when he completed his graduate degree.

Pongpol liked the idea of working in a financial services firm. While he had enjoyed his work back in Thailand in the bank, a financial services firm offered more prestige, and the opportunity to earn more money. He interviewed with a number of firms, however, the only offer he received was the one from Premuris. Marianne had presented a very bright picture of the opportunites for him in the firm, including the opportunity to advance into a managerial position within two years. It was with great excitement that Pongpol accepted the position with Premuris.

At first Marianne felt that the choice of Pongpol had been the correct one. Pongpol was very friendly with everyone in the office, he seemed eager to learn the financial services business, and he was very respectful to Marianne. Marianne tried to learn something about Thai culture including the typical Thai greeting of a wai. In the morning Marianne sometimes greeted Pongpol by pressing her fingers together as if to pray, and then bowed her head. She was surprised by Pongpol's reaction. Expecting to receive a wai from him in return she instead simply received a smile and some brief laughter. It appeared to her that Pongpol was uncomfortable with the traditional Thai greeting. Marianne, unlike others in the office refused to refer to Pongpol by his nickname, Moo, when she discovered it meant pig in Thai.

The Wrong Choice?

As time passed Marianne began to question her decision to hire Pongpol. The first indication that her decision may have been a wrong one involved excessive requests from Pongpol for time off from work for various social activities. Although Pongpol was still viewed as motivated to learn his job, Marianne was disheartened at his frequent requests to miss work. On one occasion Pongpol had requested three days off since his family was visiting from Thailand and he wanted to show them the various tourist sites of Southern California. His family had never been to the United States, and so she understood Pongpol's desire to make their visit enjoyable, however, she was completely taken aback when Pongpol asked for an additional two days to take them to Las Vegas. Marianne agreed that Pongpol could take three days off but refused to allow the additional two days for a trip to Vegas. Pongpol surprised and angered her when he did not report for work on those two days. Because of his perceived importance to the firm, Marianne decided to let this go, however, she wondered if further acts of insubordination would follow. It wasn't long before additional problems, did in fact, occur.

Marianne had decided that in order to motivate the new hires, including Pongpol, she should develop a small award program. She decided that a contest would be held in which the new employees would be treated to a dinner honoring all of them, and tickets to an L.A. Lakers game would be given to the highest performing new recruit. Pongpol didn't seem very interested in the contest, and in fact, made some derogative comments about the whole process. When the contest had ended Pongpol had not won, however, as agreed, he was invited to the dinner honoring a good effort by all the new recruits. Pongpol did not attend, instead, opting to take Stacy to a new Thai restaurant which had recently opened in the area. Pongpol was the only new recruit not to attend the event.

During the early months of his employment Marianne became concerned with Pongpol's success in generating new business for Premuris. He seemed to have made little progress in developing contacts in the Thai community that resulted in business for the firm. Marianne decided that Pongpol should be coached, and so she began to work more closely with him. Marianne had noticed that Pongpol frequently spent time socializing with others at work and reading magazines in the company lunchroom. When she asked about his behavior, Pongpol smiled and told her it was simply "sunuk" and that he would work harder to meet her expectations. Marianne was confused but reassured that Pongpol seemed to be indicating that he would work harder.

After the fourth month, Marianne's patience with Pongpol began to fade. Increasingly she grew angry at his apparent lack of seriousness with his work and his lack of success in generating new business for the firm. On one occasion Marianne found Pongpol reading what appeared to be a martial arts magazine at his desk. She proceeded to tell him that he better begin to take his work more seriously, and that it appeared he was simply lazy and unwilling to do what was necessary in order to generate new business. Marianne's voice was loud, and it was clear that everyone around the two of them heard the entire conversation. For the next two weeks Pongpol was busy making calls from his desk, but he was very cool towards

Marianne. It was rumored that Pongpol had developed an unflattering nickname for Marianne that translated in English to "hot heart." Marianne was not sure what this meant and she seemed unconcerned with the label. It then came as a big surprise to Marianne when Pongpol invited her to his home for a Thai dinner. Thinking that this might be a good way to gain his respect, Marianne eagerly accepted the invitation.

The King's Birthday

Marianne learned that Pongpol was having the dinner on the King of Thailand's birthday so she decided to purchase a copy of the movie *Anna and the King* to give to Pongpol as a present when she came for dinner. On the night of the dinner Marianne arrived at Pongpol's home with the movie and received a warm welcome from Pongpol and Stacy. Marianne noticed that neither of the two, nor the other guests were wearing shoes and she thought this odd, however, she soon forgot about it as she began to notice the finely carved wood pieces in the apartment. Most of the decorations were of elephants and she spent much time admiring the objects. Pongpol explained that the elephant was an important symbol in Thailand and that the Thai people were in general very fond of the animal. Marianne also noticed a large picture of a man in royal attire whom Pongpol told her was the king of his country.

During dinner Pongpol explained all of the various dishes. Marianne enjoyed learning about Thai food and appreciated most of the dishes, even though she felt the food was very spicy. She felt uncomfortable sitting on the floor eating and also eating with others who had no shoes, but she felt that the experience would provide the opportunity to better understand Pongpol and his culture. Marianne learned much about the personal side of Pongpol at dinner. For example, she learned that he practiced kickboxing, a sport she knew very little about, and that he had a rather large tattoo of a tiger on his arm. Marianne also learned that Pongpol and Stacy liked to travel to Las Vegas on weekends and that Pongpol was fond of gambling, and somewhat skilled at the game of blackjack.

As the night progressed the discussion turned to Marianne. She told of her background and seemed to become more relaxed as she consumed more alcohol. Marianne told Pongpol and Stacy that she was of British decent and that she felt royalty served no purpose in Great Britain anymore, other than to produce "royal scandals," and that she was surprised to learn that Thailand still had a king. Looking at the picture of the King of Thailand in Pongpol's apartment, Marianne commented that the king looked "kind of nerdy." At that moment Marianne remembered the gift she had brought and proceeded to retrieve it from her bag and give it to Pongpol. Pongpol smiled, thanked her for the gift, and set it aside. Marianne insisted that he open the gift which he did and his reaction was less than she had expected. He just smiled and thanked her again without any comment on the film or how he might enjoy watching it. It seemed at this point that it was a good time to end the evening and Marianne thanked Pongpol and Stacy and left for home. Marianne felt that the evening went well as she drove home. Although there seemed to be some strange reactions and tensions at times, Marianne felt that the dinner had given her the opportunity to get to know Pongpol better and that this may help her better motivate him to improve his performance.

Ride Him Like an Elephant

During the next two weeks there really didn't seem to be any change in Pongpol's behavior. He still spent too much time out of the office, continued to read his martial arts magazines at work, and had not produced much new business for the firm. Marianne's criticism of him became increasingly hostile and loud. She had hoped that if she ridiculed him in public that he would be motivated to work harder in order to avoid "losing face." She knew that the concept of face saving was important in Asian societies. At first it appeared that her approach was working. Pongpol spent more time in the office, stopped reading his magazines at work, and informed Marianne that he had acquired a very sizable new account from a wealthy Thai businessman. Marianne felt that the only way to motivate Pongpol was to "ride him like an elephant." Increasingly Marianne pressured Pongpol in public to produce more new accounts, and it did seem to pay off. Pongpol was generating new business, in fact, the revenue from the one new account was expected to exceed the revenue from all the new accounts produced from the other four new financial services advisors, and he had managed to acquire some smaller accounts as well.

At the end of six months it was time for Pongpol's performance appraisal. Marianne had asked him to schedule a time when they could meet for the appraisal. Pongpol never responded, and so, Marianne instead set a date and time for the meeting. She was outraged when Pongpol did not show up for the meeting and could not be found anywhere in the office. When he did finally arrive in the office later that day, Marianne demanded to see him in her office. She flew into a fit of rage and proceeded to detail all of Pongpol's perceived deficiencies. After a long, and loud assessment of his weaknesses Pongpol remained silent. When asked why he did not show up for the scheduled meeting, Pongpol just smiled and nervously laughed. He had no explanation. Marianne told Pongpol to leave her office, that she would discuss his performance with her manager, and that a decision would be made concerning Pongpol's future with the company.

As Pongpol left the office, Marianne sat at her desk for a moment and then telephoned Bill Nestbaum, her manager. Marianne immediately began to explain her difficulties with Pongpol to Bill. Bill listened patiently and then proceeded to tell Marianne that he was just about to call her to congratulate her on Pongpol's new account. After some confusion over which account he was referring to, Marianne learned that Pongpol had just opened an account for another wealthy Thai businessperson, one that was expected to be much larger in fact than the earlier large account Pongpol had acquired.

Marianne wasn't sure what to say to Bill at this point. She quickly ended the telephone call and sat in her office staring out her window. She began to review the entire situation in her mind and to ponder her next move. Marianne thought aloud to herself that managing Pongpol was like trying to dance with an elephant, and she was not sure how she should proceed with this dance.

SOURCES

Gannon, M. (2001). <u>Working across cultures</u>. Thousand Oaks, CA: Sage Publications.

Goodman, J. (1996). <u>Cultures of the world: Thailand</u>. New York: Marshall Cavendish.

Koehler, H. (1994). <u>Kiss, bow, or shake hands</u>. Holbrook, MA: Adams Media.

Mead, R. (1998). <u>International management</u>. Malden, MA: Blackwell Publishers.

McNair, S. (1998). <u>Thailand</u>. New York: Grolier Publishing.

Scarborough, J. (2001). <u>The origins of cultural differences and their impact on management</u>. Westport, CT: Quorum Books.

Wise, N. (1997). <u>Passport Thailand</u>. San Rafael, CA: World Trade Press.

<u>WWW.countrywatch.com/Thailand</u>. Retrieved December 14, 2001.

<u>WWW.state.gov</u>. Background notes: Thailand. Retrieved January 2, 2002.

This case was prepared by Charles A. Rarick.

CASE 6

AN AMERICAN GAUCHO IN ARGENTINA

ABSTRACT

Peter Fuller, an American executive with Great Plains Foods of Iowa travels to Buenos Aires to investigate the possibility of forming a strategic alliance with Comidas Gaucho, an Argentine beef processor. While the potential gains from the alliance appear to be great for both companies, difficulties develop during the business trip that cause Peter to reconsider the potential relationship.

As Peter Fuller returned to his hotel room in the capital of Argentina he could not get a song out of his head that he had heard earlier that evening. Peter had been invited for a night out on the town with his new Argentine business associates and he had experienced an evening of tango and great music. The evening went well, and he especially like the song *Mi Noche Triste* or as he was told, translated in English to *My Sad Night*. Peter began to think back over his brief visit to Argentina and how the business trip had not produced the results he had hoped.

Great Plains Foods

Headquartered in Osceola, Iowa, Great Plains Foods, Inc. is a manufacturer and marketer of consumer branded meat products. Hans Mueller, a German immigrant when he was only nineteen years old, founded the company in 1896. The company began processing pork products and later expanded into other meat products. Hans retired in 1945 and his son William became president and chief executive officer until 1991 when he died of a heart attack. William's son, Christian succeeded his father and managed to keep Great Plains a family business. The company operates manufacturing facilities in five states and Great Plains products can be found in retail shelves in all 50 states. Since 1994 Great Plains has embarked on an aggressive export strategy and now sells in over 10 countries under the Great Plains brand, and a few other lesser-known brand names. As part of the aggressive international expansion, Great Plains also began to seek foreign sourcing for its products.

Peter Fuller Arrives in Buenos Aires

Through a series of contacts, Great Plains was able to establish a meeting with the leading food processor in Argentina, Comidas Gaucho. A three-day business trip was planned in which Peter Fuller, a senior vice president of Great Plains would meet with Comidas Gaucho representatives to discuss a possible strategic alliance between the two companies. Peter had never been in Argentina and he eagerly anticipated the trip.

The trip to Argentina began on a hot day in July. Peter boarded his flight for Buenos Aires, which stopped in Miami. By the time Peter arrived at Ezeiza International airport in Buenos Aires he was exhausted, yet he hoped to get as much out of the trip as possible, and he looked forward to meeting the representatives of Comidas Gaucho. During the flight Peter reviewed the documents which he was going to present to Comidas, detailing the proposed strategic alliance. He was anxious to discuss the ways in which the two companies could cooperate.

As Peter waited for his luggage he mentally rehearsed what he was going to tell the Comidas representatives. He retrieved his luggage and made his way through customs and immigration and stepped outside the airport. Peter was surprised to see people wearing coats in the airport, after all, it was July and it was South America! Peter was wearing a short-shelve knit shirt and found it to be insufficient protection for the weather he had not anticipated. It was "hot in Miami and cold here," Peter thought to himself. It must just be some freakish weather today in Buenos Aires he thought. The cool temperature left his head as he noticed a smiling young man holding a sign with his name on it. Peter was met by Jorge Antonio Martinez, a representative of Comidas Gaucho. The two men exchanged greetings and then proceeded to go to Jorge's automobile. Peter was very pleased by the warmth and friendliness of Jorge and he thought to himself that doing business in Argentina would be easy. Peter was somewhat taken aback when Jorge asked him if he enjoyed the beach in Miami. "Why is he asking me about a beach. Doesn't he know that I came straight here for business," Peter thought. After some discussion Peter learned that Jorge was commenting on his wardrobe. Still a bit confused, Peter concluded that it was meant to be a joke. Jorge dropped Peter off at his hotel and told him that he would be coming by at 10 P.M. to take him for dinner. Peter thought to himself that he had planned to be in bed by then but that he could adjust to the late invitation.

Peter checked into his room, unpacked his luggage, and decided to get some rest. Later in the evening Jorge escorted Peter to one of the finest restaurants in Buenos Aires. Peter had hoped that he would be meeting Juan Garcia, the CEO of Comidas, but Jorge informed him that Senor Garcia would be meeting him in the morning. Peter wasn't really sure of Jorge's influence in the company, yet he decided to go ahead with his plan and to begin to discuss the alliance proposal with Jorge. Each time Peter brought up the subject Jorge politely changed the topic. After a number of attempts, Peter decided that Jorge wasn't a significant enough player in the company and that he would instead discuss other topics with him over dinner. After discussing the weather in Argentina, the differences in Argentine wine, and a variety of other subjects of little interest to Peter, he decided that he would tell Jorge about his British uncle who had fought in the Falklands. After all, the dinner topics were not very interesting and it appeared that Jorge had no intention of ending the evening anytime soon. Peter knew that the subject may be somewhat sensitive, however, it was many years ago and he reasoned that Jorge might find it interesting. As Peter described the stories his uncle told him Jorge sat quietly, puffing on his cigarette and staring at Peter. After a few minutes Jorge interrupted Peter and told him a polite, but firm tone that the issue was a very sensitive one for most Argentines and that it would be best if he studied the facts of the situation and learned the proper name of the islands before he engaged others in this topic.

The two men sipped some more wine and Jorge continued to smoke, and make some jokes about Peter who was a non-smoker and "North Americans who think they can live forever." Peter explained how it was now considered rude in the United States to smoke in the presence of others without asking first for permission. Jorge chuckled a bit and told Peter it was a good thing that he didn't live in the United States. After the dinner had ended Jorge returned Peter to his hotel and told him that he would return at about 10 A.M. to take him to the offices of Comidas. At that moment Peter remembered that he had brought gifts for the Comidas representatives and he ran up to his room to get one for Jorge. Peter gave Jorge a box that was neatly gift-wrapped. Inside the box was a set of premium steak knives that Great Plains Foods frequently gave as a gift to potential customers. Jorge thanked Peter for the gift without opening it and excused himself for the evening. Peter returned to his room feeling that, with the exception of the Falklands discussion, the night had gone well. He looked at the clock in his room and decided that it was too late to phone his wife. Peter was looking forward to finally discussing business in the morning.

A Bitter Taste in the Offices

Peter arose early the next morning and ate breakfast in his room as he prepared for his meeting with Juan Garcia. He was preparing to deliver a presentation on the many benefits Comidas would have with its association with Great Plains Foods. Great Plains would provide the brand name and marketing expertise and Comidas could provide the meat products and processing for a rapid expansion into the South American markets.

Peter went down to the hotel lobby at 9:45 A.M. and waited for Jorge to arrive. While Peter was anxious to get to the offices, he realized that time in Latin America was somewhat different than he was use to in Iowa and so he didn't become concerned when he looked at his watch and it was 10:15AM. By 10:30 A.M. Peter began to worry and decided to call Jorge on the cell phone number that was printed on Jorge's business card. Jorge told Peter that he was running a little late and that he would be there in about 10 minutes. At 10:45 A.M. Peter again called Jorge, this time expressing his concern about not being on time for his meeting with Mr. Garcia. Jorge told him everything was fine and that he would be there very soon. Jorge arrived a little after 11:00 A.M. and apologized to Peter for being late. The traffic was worse than normal he explained, and he reassured Peter that everyone would understand.

The ride to the offices was a bit tense as Peter was very unhappy that he would arrive late for the meeting with Mr. Garcia and that this might make him look bad. Jorge tried to change the mood by engaging Peter in talk of politics and sports, but Peter was too focused on the meeting to care. Jorge was an avid soccer fan and wanted to tell Peter about the national team. Peter did not seem too interested. After a short ride the two men arrived at the headquarters of Comidas. The offices were located behind a large wire fence and Peter noticed that there were many guards and that some of them had guns. This made him wonder about Argentina and about Comidas.

Once inside the offices Peter was impressed with the company's facilities. The office of Comidas Gaucho was more elaborate and ornate than his own company headquarters. The lobby, with its marble floors and crystal light fixtures featured a large horse statute. Peter took a few minutes to look around the lobby and to take in its splendor. Anna Lopez, administrative assistant to Mr. Garcia, interrupted his thought. Anna welcomed Peter to the company and inquired about his flight and his first impressions of the country. The two made small talk for a few minutes and then Peter quickly changed the subject telling Anna that he was late for his appointment with Mr. Garcia and that he was worried that he was keeping him waiting. Anna explained that everything was fine, and that Mr. Garcia had an unexpected appointment which was going to make him a little late for their meeting. She invited Peter to the offices upstairs to wait for Mr. Garcia.

After waiting for about 30 minutes Peter was approached by a middle-aged man, handsomely dressed, who introduced himself as Juan Garcia. Peter noticed the tailored suit, silk tie, and cuff links on the company's CEO and contrasted this wardrobe to what he, Peter, was wearing. Peter had assumed that business would be more casual in South America, and so he decided that a sports coat, without a tie would be appropriate. Suddenly he felt underdressed. Mr. Garcia greeted Peter with a firm handshake and told him how happy he was to have him visit the company. While Mr. Garcia spoke English, it appeared to Peter that he was not totally fluent.

Mr. Garcia invited Peter to join him in his office. Once inside the office Mr. Garcia asked Peter if he would like some mate. Peter wasn't sure what he was being offered and so he declined. After all, the meeting was running behind schedule and Peter was anxious to explain what he had to offer Comidas Gaucho. Peter thanked Mr. Garcia for inviting him down to discuss the possibilities for the two companies and then gave Mr. Garcia the gift of steak knives and a report that he had prepared. The report explained in great detail how the two companies could benefit from Peter's planned partnership. Mr. Garcia briefly glanced at the report and then proceeded to ask Peter about his family. The discussion was interrupted by a secretary, who brought into the office what appeared to be a hollowed-out gourd with a very large straw, and offered it to Peter. Peter thanked her as Mr. Garcia explained that it was a traditional Argentine herbal drink. Peter took one sip and decided that it wasn't to his liking. The two men discussed world politics and their two companies, but Peter was never able to get around to his proposal. After about an hour, Mr. Garcia's secretary interrupted the meeting again by saying something in Spanish, and Mr. Garcia told Peter that it had been very nice to meet him, and that he now wanted Peter to speak with the vice president of international operations.

Peter was escorted to the office of Eduardo Guillermo, a young Argentine man with an excellent command of the English language. Eduardo had studied in the United States and appeared eager to discuss Peter's proposal. Peter reasoned that Eduardo would explain to Mr. Garcia how the plan would work. Peter explained to Eduardo that Great Plains was offering Comidas the use of its well-received brand name and marketing expertise for expansion into the South American market. Eduardo appeared very interested and told Peter that Comidas could offer the advantage of MERCOUSUR, the customs union involving the countries of Argentina, Brazil, Paraguay, and Uruguay. Peter really wasn't sure of this advantage, and proceeded to tell Eduardo that Comidas could provide the meat distribution and processing, and that the two companies could share in the venture in an equal fashion. Peter explained to Eduardo how Great Plains was interested in a rapid expansion into the South American market. Eduardo explained how the market had potential but that he wasn't sure consumers would respond to the Great Plains brand. Eduardo also hinted to the possibility that the financial requirements needed for the association may be too great for Comidas at this time. The two men talked for some time until Eduardo told Peter that there were a few other people he should meet in the company. Peter spent the remaining part of that Friday afternoon discussing his proposal with various other Comidas executives. At the end of the afternoon Eduardo drove Peter back to his hotel and told him that he would have the opportunity to discuss the idea further with Mr. Garcia at the company asado or barbecue tomorrow. Peter ate dinner in the hotel restaurant that evening, telephoned his wife, and went to bed early.

Being Roasted at an Asado

Peter was happy to accept the invitation from Eduardo to attend the barbeque, as he thought this might be an opportunity to further discuss business, and perhaps build better relations with Mr. Garcia. Eduardo gave Peter the directions, apologized to Peter that no one would be able to take him, and explained that he would have to take a taxi to the event. Peter was given directions to Mr. Garcia's house and told to arrive at one in the afternoon.

Realizing that events rarely begin on time, Peter arrived at two o'clock and was dressed for the event, or so he thought. He had purchased an entire gaucho outfit for the event. Peter was dressed from head-to-toe as an Argentine cowboy and greeted the other guests with a big smile. While he had found the employees of Comidas very friendly at the offices, he felt that they were being somewhat distant to him at the barbeque. Many guests greeted each other with a kiss, and there was a lot of kissing he thought, but not for him. He greeted many people and make small talk with a few people. Most people commented on his outfit and seemed to find it amusing. Peter noticed that he was the last person to arrive at the barbecue.

Peter had hoped that he would have an opportunity to discuss business in greater depth with Mr. Garcia at the event but it appeared that Mr. Garcia was avoiding him. It also appeared to Peter that Jorge was avoiding him as well. Peter finally found Eduardo who welcomed him and the two began to discuss the proposal. Again Eduardo expressed his concerns about the agreement, and Peter again tried to explain how the proposal clearly showed that both companies would benefit from the partnership. Not really sure of why Eduardo was not enthusiastic about the proposal, Peter feared that perhaps Comidas was worried that their Latin American customers would not appreciate the American brand. At that moment Peter remembered how Great Plains had been able to successfully launch a marketing campaign in the United States on Spanish language television aimed at the Hispanic market. Peter told Eduardo about the campaign, but Eduardo still didn't seem convinced.

As the barbecue appeared to be winding down Mr. Garcia began making some toasts. While he was speaking Spanish, and Peter didn't understand what he was saying, he did reason that it was very cordial. Towards the end of the toasting Peter hear a few words that he understood including "amigo de los Estados Unidos" and he knew that Mr. Garcia was referring to him. The toasts went on for some time with great laughter from the crowd. Peter finally turned to Eduardo for an explanation. Eduardo told Peter that Mr. Garcia was talking about him and "just making some jokes." Eduardo assured Peter that there was really no problem. At the end of the event Eduardo informed Peter that he and Jorge would be taking Peter out for a night on the town to enjoy Argentine culture. While Peter appreciated the offer, he knew that he had to at some point again see Mr. Garcia. Peter was finally able to reach Mr. Garcia and thanked him for inviting him to the barbecue. Mr. Garcia thanked Peter for coming and told him that he looked forward to more discussion on the ways the two companies could do business. Peter was a bit worried in that he was scheduled to leave for Iowa in the morning.

The evening with Jorge and Eduardo was filled with great food, wine, and song. Peter enjoyed the company of the two men and he was able to again discuss his proposal with them. The two men seemed genuinely interested in the ideas but they stopped short of offering any advice or assessments. Finally Peter asked Eduardo directly why it appeared that the proposal was not being accepted. Eduardo said that there was really not any big problem with the proposal, and that he thought the two companies could in fact work together in the future. Eduardo suggested that he come to Iowa and visit Great Plains and discuss further the prospects for cooperation. While agreeing with Eduardo about the idea that he visit Great Plains, Peter felt that the business trip was not a success, and that there was little chance that the partnership would materialize.

SOURCES

Campbell, A. (2000). <u>Passport Argentina</u>. Novato, CA: World Trade Press.
Frank, N. (2000). <u>Argentina</u>. Milwaukee: Gareth Stevens Publishing.
Hintz, M. (1998). <u>Argentina</u>. New York: Grolier Publishing.
Morrison, T., Conaway, W., and G. Borden. (1994). <u>Kiss, Bow, or Shake Hands</u>. Holbrook, MA: Adams Media.

This case was prepared by Charles A. Rarick.

EXERCISE 1

WHO AM I?

Purpose: The purpose of this exercise is to show the importance different cultural groups place on different aspects of their identity.

Procedure: Draw a circle on a piece of paper and construct a pie chart that describes your identity with different groups to which you belong. Examples may include male, white, Christian, mom/dad, American, employee, etc. The classification is your decision.

Show the degree of importance of each group affiliation by the size of the slice in your diagram.

EXERCISE 2

CROSS-CULTURAL QUIZ

Purpose: The purpose of this exercise is to test your knowledge of different aspects of culture in selected countries.

Procedure: Answer the 30 questions that follow. After you have answered all the questions your instructor will provide you with the correct answers.

1. ____ In Saudi Arabia, it is important to use your left hand when passing important documents to your business host.

2. ____ Germans have a relaxed sense to time and, therefore, business meetings seldom start on schedule.

3. ____ Australian culture is one of the most individualistic in the world.

4. ____ The Japanese generally stand further apart than the Americans when communicating.

5. ____ Thais generally appreciate a frank and open evaluation of their performance.

6. ____ Gift giving in Vietnam is very common in business, and

the use of white wrapping paper shows your respect for the recipient.

7. ___ Mexican businesspeople have a relaxed sense of dress and, therefore, will not expect their visitors to dress formally when conducting business.

8. ___ Russians are known for their moodiness and stoic manner.

9. ___ Israelis are known for being some of the most courteous drivers in the world.

10. ___ In Poland, education is highly valued and one's status is directly related to their educational achievement.

11. ___ Duty to family is an important Indian value, and workers in India will often expect workplace concessions to be made for family matters.

12. ___ Calling someone a "tico" in Costa Rica is considered an insult.

13. ___ A favorite pastime of the French is the cinema.

14. ___ The colors of the Indian flag (red, white, green) represent the three major religions of India.

15. ___ The Chinese value their privacy, therefore, asking questions of a personal nature such as age or marital status will be seen as bad manners.

16. ___ A handshake and a verbal agreement carry the same weight in Argentina as a written agreement.

17. ___ French organizations tend to be centralized, hierarchical, and formal.

18. ___ Because of their strong individualistic nature, most Costa Ricans prefer to work independently.

19. ___ Kosher foods in Israel include ham, lobster, and a cheeseburger.

20. ___ Poles are very time-oriented and will seldom be late for an appointment.

21. ___ Contracts are not viewed as final agreements by many Russian businesspeople.

22. ____ When passing through a doorway, it is customary for African men to enter before women.

23. ____ Most Thais give great deference to superiors and would be unlikely to question a directive.

24. ____ In Vietnam, because there are few surnames, people are commonly addressed by their given names.

25. ____ Russians often say "nyet" or no to a proposal, even if they consider it to be a good one.

26. ____ The communication style of most South Africans is very flexible, and frequent interruptions are not considered rude.

27. ____ In China, the traditional color of weddings is red, and the color white is reserved for funerals.

28. ____ Thais are generally seen as friendly people, and will often hug and kiss strangers upon meeting.

29. ____ The people of Belgium are considered to be the most health conscious in the world and have a particular dislike of French fries.

30. ____ Argentina stands out from its neighbors in its intolerance for corruption.

EXERCISE 3

CULTURE RANKING EXERCISE

Purpose: To develop a better understanding of cultural differences and how they affect international management. This exercise uses the model developed by cross-cultural researcher Geert Hofstede and tests your knowledge of ten different cultures.

Procedure: Read the brief description of each element of Hofstede's framework and individually rank each of the listed countries from high to low on the four dimensions of the model. The country highest on a dimension receives a ranking of 1, and the country lowest on the dimension receives a 10. Assemble into groups and discuss your rankings. As a group, develop another ranking, again using 1 = highest and 10 = lowest. Finally, answer as a group the four questions at the end of the exercise.

Hofstede Model:

Working with IBM employees, Danish psychologist Geert Hofstede discovered four dimensions on which cultures differ. Although the sample was limited in terms of representation (employees of IBM), it was an extensive empirical study of individuals from many different cultures, and it stands as the most popular cross-cultural framework involving managerial issues. Hofstede discovered that cultures differ in terms of power distance (PD), uncertainty avoidance (UA), masculinity-femininity (M), and individualism-collectivism (I).

INDIVIDUAL RANKING

COUNTRIES	PD	UA	M	I
France				
Great Britain				
Guatemala				
Israel				
Jamaica				
Japan				
Mexico				
Pakistan				
Sweden				
USA				

GROUP RANKING

COUNTRIES	PD	UA	M	I
France				
Great Britain				
Guatemala				
Israel				
Jamaica				
Japan				
Mexico				
Pakistan				
Sweden				
USA				

Questions: 1. In which countries should managers find a participative approach to management most effective? In which countries would such an approach be less effective?

2. In which countries would you expect to find a greater emphasis on training and developing the workforce?

3. In which countries would you expect supervisors to provide specific instructions to their employees?

4. In which countries would teamwork be an effective management practice? Which countries do you think would have the greatest difficulty implementing a team approach?

EXERCISE 4

CULTURAL METAPHORS

Purpose: The purpose of this exercise is to develop an appreciation of the use of metaphors in understanding cultural values.

Procedure: Read the background material that follows and select a country in which you would like to learn more about. Do not select a country that is discussed in the background information.

Investigate the national culture of the country you selected and develop a metaphor which, in your opinion, best describes that culture. Two examples are provided in the background information.

Background: Gannon (2001) proposed metaphor analysis as a more content-rich approach to describing cultures. The metaphor highlights dimensions important to a culture.

Examples of country metaphors could include:

Germany – German Symphony Orchestra

- Individual musicians must be highly talented and trained.
- A successful German symphony requires a skilled leader
- Precision and synchronicity are critical

United States – Marlboro Man

- The Marlboro man is a rugged individual
- He is self-sufficient and doesn't like to ask for help
- He tends to be aggressive and an achiever

This exercise was inspired by M. Gannon (2001). <u>Understanding Global Cultures: Metaphorical Journeys Through 23 Countries</u>.
Thousand Oaks, CA: Sage Publishers.

PART TWO

CROSS-CULTURAL COMMUNICATION AND NEGOTIATION

We have seen the impact of cultural differences on international business and management. International managers and entrepreneurs can improve their international success by improving their ability to understand and appreciate other cultures. This cultural awareness helps managers adjust their attitudes and behaviors, and ultimately makes them more effective in dealing with different cultural environments. Cultural awareness requires managers to improve their communication skills and cultural empathy. The following cases show the impacts of culture and the importance of cross cultural communication, conflict, and negotiation.

Cases:
Canada Timber
Anne Burn's Personal Jihad
Kidnapped In Colombia

Exercises:
Cultural Filters in Perception
Cross-Cultural Negotiations

CASE 7

CANADA TIMBER

Logging Time Negotiating with the Japanese

ABSTRACT

A Canadian team of negotiators travel to Japan to meet with a potential customer and to bring back a contract. The meetings do not go well, and the Canadians are left wondering what they could have done differently in order to have gained the trust of their Japanese hosts.

Introduction

Tim Wilder, CEO of Canada Timber was excited as he hung up the telephone in his office in Vancouver, British Colombia. Tim had just received a call from Akiko Morita, who represented the Japanese furniture manufacturer, Bonsai. Morita informed Tim that Canada Timber was being considered as a major supplier to Bonsai. He told Tim that Canada Timber's reputation as a supplier of quality hardwoods was of interest to Bonsai their Japanese customers. Canada Timber exported its products to the United States, Mexico, and several European countries, however, the company did not have any customers anywhere in Asia. Tim was excited about the prospect of exporting to Asia.

After several long distance telephone calls and several more faxes, it was decided that Tim and two of his associates would travel to Japan in order to close an initial sales contract. In addition, Tim asked his attorney brother-in-law, Johnny Sharkey to accompany them, and to act as their legal representative. Tim selected a production supervisor from Canada Timber, and another member of management to accompany him on the long journey. Bill Hudak, production supervisor was a long-term employee of Canada Timber. His knowledge of hardwoods and the production procedures of Canada Timber made him an obvious choice, Tim reasoned, for inclusion on the negotiating team. Tim also asked Kevin Peterson to go along, since Kevin was married to a woman of Japanese decent, and Tim felt he would make a good impression on the Japanese. None of the Canada Timber employees, or Johnny spoke Japanese. Kevin knew a few words in Japanese and was somewhat familiar with Japanese culture.

The Japanese had faxed a number of documents to Tim concerning the meetings. Tim was very impressed with the degree of detail provided by the Japanese, including the names and qualifications of the people they would meet during their visit to Japan. A detailed agenda was provided, and the Japanese made all arrangements for transportation and lodging for the Canadians.

Arriving in Japan

After an exhausting flight, the Canadians arrived in Japan and were greeted by Akiko Morita and other representatives of Bonsai. The Japanese bowed and handed Tim their business cards. Tim, exhausted from the flight, took the business cards from each Bonsai representative and quickly stuffed them into his shirt pocket. After a brief conversation, the Bonsai employees took the Canadians to their hotel to rest. They would be back in the morning to escort them to Bonsai headquarters. The Canadians were very tired but excited to be in Japan. They rested a bit, and then spent the rest of the afternoon and early evening walking the streets of Tokyo.

When Tim and his associates arrived at Bonsai headquarters they were presented with a gift from the company president Mr. Kenichi Kusushi. John was unsure if he should open the gift or not, so he decided to thank Mr. Kusushi for the gift and to stuff it into his briefcase. Once again a number of business cards were presented to John and the others, and at this point, Tim remembered that he had forgotten to bring his business cards along. He apologized for the oversight and once again quickly collected the cards from the Japanese.

The meeting began with Mr. Kusushi asking, through an interpreter, how the Canadians liked Japan so far. Tim and the others expressed an appreciation for being in the country and pointed out that Kevin had been to Japanese previously while visiting the family of his Japanese wife. The Japanese remained silent as the Canadians told of how they had explored the city the night before and commented on how crowded the city was compared to Vancouver. Tim, who is a very tall man, stated that he felt like a "giant among men in Japan."

It appeared to Tim that the Japanese were very interested in the Canadian's perceptions of the country, and that they would begin to discuss business if he would offer some complements. Tim thought about the situation and offered some positive comments on the food and drink they had enjoyed in their hotel. Tim then quickly began to discuss business, pointing out how Canada Timber was a quality leader in supplying hardwood products to several countries. He went on at great length about the positive attributes of his company and how it would be a good business decision to select Canada Timber as a supplier.

Seal the Deal

Bonsai had faxed some preliminary estimates of their wood needs and Tim had prepared a detailed report that he presented at the meeting. At the end of the report Tim provided details on costs, and then asked Mr. Kusushi if the number were acceptable. A long period of silence began. Tim and the other Canadians began to feel a bit nervous after a few moments had passed and he again asked, through the translator, if the price was acceptable. Mr. Kusushi smiled and laughed a bit without saying a word. He then looked to one of the members of the Japanese negotiating team and the two spoke in Japanese without the conversation being translated. At this point Tim interrupted by saying that perhaps the price could be a bit lower if needed. More silence followed and Tim became increasingly nervous. He began to speak, this time addressing the translator and asking if anything could be done to "seal the deal today." He pulled a contract out of his briefcase, lowered the price by 10% and asked Johnny to explain the important points of the sales contract. Mr. Kusushi sat quietly as Johnny explained the details of the contract to the Japanese. Tim and Johnny were concerned that Mr. Kusushi did not say much and that he never made good eye contact with them. After the details of the contract were explained, one of the more senior Japanese representatives suggested that the group take a short break. Tim thought this was a good sign and agreed. He stood up to shake the hand of each Japanese employee as they left the room. When he approached Mr. Kusushi, he gave an especially firm handshake and a pat on the shoulder. He told Mr. Kusushi, referring to him as Kenichi, that he was certain the two could work out a favorable arrangement, and that Canada Timber was prepared to do whatever was necessary in order to become a Bonsai supplier.

When the meeting resumed, Tim was informed that he and his associates were invited to tour one of Bonsai's manufacturing plants, which was located a few hours from Tokyo. Tim happily accepted the invitation, and the Canadians were off to the plant. After much formality once arriving at the plant, the Canadians were given an extensive tour. Tim and Bill Hudak asked many questions about the operation and they felt that they now had a better understanding of the material requirements needed by Bonsai. After the plant tour, the Canadians were taken back to their hotel and told that a Bonsai representative would pick them up in the morning and bring them back to company headquarters.

That evening the four men discussed what had happened during the day and how they should proceed. Kevin felt that everything was on schedule for the Japanese and that it would simply take more time in order to close the deal. He explained that silence was a negotiating tactic of the Japanese, and that Tim should not make any more concession on price. Tim agreed that the price was already low and that not much profit would be made. However, he felt that if he could get the Japanese to sign a contract, and that if they liked the product, they would be able to do further business under better financial conditions. The four men generally agreed that they should seek a commitment from the Japanese in the morning.

The Final Offer

The following day, however, would be no more successful for Tim and his team. After many hours of explaining once again how Canada Timber was the right choice, and that the price was very low, Tim was beginning to get frustrated. He felt that the Japanese were holding out for a lower price, and so he decided to offer a 15% reduction in order to end the negotiations. After the offer Tim slouched down in his chair and decided that he would use silence to his advantage. Tim sat silently and stared at Mr. Kusushi. It seemed like an eternity to the Canadians when someone from the Japanese side finally spoke. One of the senior Japanese employees suggested that the negotiations end for the day and that they resume the following morning. He further suggested that all members of the two teams go out in the evening to experience Japanese culture. At first Tim thought that he could take no further delays, but he then reasoned that he might be able to reach an agreement with the Japanese in a more informal setting.

During dinner Tim continued to press Mr. Kusushi for a decision. Mr. Kusushi politely said that he thought Canada Timber would be a good partner for Bonsai, yet made no commitment. After dinner the Japanese took the Canadians to a very popular bar in Tokyo and all participants drank heavily. After a few hours Tim moved close to Mr. Kusushi, put his arm around his neck and told him that he was his new friend. Tim told Kusushi that he was going to give his new friend the best price he possibly could and that meant that he was going to make a final offer of a price reduction of 20%, if he would agree to the deal right now. Mr. Kusushi laughed and responded in English "yes." Tim was finally convinced that the team had closed the deal and that a contract would be signed in the morning.

Just One More Day

On the following morning Tim had Johnny prepare a revised sales agreement with the discounted price. Although the price was much lower than Tim had hoped for, and near his breakeven point, Tim, nevertheless, felt that a long-term association with Bonsai and the potential for additional sales in Asia would be beneficial to the company. He was also happy to be able to return to Canada soon. Once again the Canadian team was met at the hotel and driven to Bonsai's headquarters. Tim entered the meeting room surprised not to find Mr. Kusushi present. When he asked the whereabouts of Mr. Kusushi he was told that he was called out of town unexpectedly and offered his apologies. Tim was told that Mr. Kusushi would return tomorrow. Tim immediately approached Akiko and told him that Mr. Kusushi had agreed to the terms listed in the sales contract he was holding in his hand. He asked if someone could sign the agreement so that he and his associates could return home. Tim was told that Mr. Kusushi would need to approve any supplier agreements and that it was impossible to do so today. Tim was very upset and it showed. His face was red and he believed that the Japanese were stalling in order to gain additional concessions. Tim moved very close to Akiko and told him that an agreement had been reached and that he should immediately telephone Mr. Kusushi to confirm. After raising his voice, Akiko telephoned Mr. Kusushi and told him of the situation. Upon his return, Akiko said, "Please excuse, Mr. Wilder-san, but we will probably need to wait just one more day." Tim, feeling that he was being manipulated stormed out of the office, and along with his negotiation team, headed for the airport.

Charles Rarick and Arifin Angriawan

SOURCES

D. Engel and K. Murakami. (2002). *Passport Japan* Novato, CA: World Trade Press.
J. Scarborough. (2000). *The Origins of Cultural Differences and Their Impact on Management*, Westport, CT: Quorum. .
R. Sanyal. (2001). *International Management*, Upper Saddle River, NJ: Prentice Hall.

This case was prepared by Charles Rarick and Gregory Winter and previously published in the International Journal of Case Studies.

CASE 8

ANNE BURN'S PERSONAL JIHAD

ABSTRACT

An American expatriate is assigned to work in a non-profit organization in Jordan that sought to promote Jordanian exports, especially those produced and sold by female entrepreneurs. She experienced difficulties as she attempted to promote the economic standing of women in Jordan, and became involved in organizational politics she did not understand.

Anne Burns, a forty-five year old American woman who started a number of businesses in the United States, was hired by a recently established non-profit organization called ExportJordan. Working with a grant from USAID, ExportJordan's mission was to further develop local businesses in Jordan in order to capitalize on the recently signed free trade agreement with the United States. Having just sold her last business, and having her two grown children out of the house, Anne and her husband, Don, decided to forgo their empty nest and strike out on a new adventure in the Middle East.

Anne and Don did not need to work since the businesses they had created, and sold, provided more than a comfortable living for them. Having many productive years ahead of them, they sought out a unique challenge. Jordan was to be that new challenge.

Jordan

Jordan is a constitutional monarchy based on heredity. Male descendants of the dynasty of King Abdullah bin al Hussein inherit the throne and rule the country without opposition. The country now called Jordan was created at the end of World War I when the League of Nations gave the territory to the United Kingdom to rule. The UK created a semi-autonomous jurisdiction called the Emirate of Transjordan. In 1946 Transjordan became an independent country and changed its name in 1950 to the Hashemite Kingdom of Jordan. The country is presently ruled by King Abdullah II, a western educated and progressive leader who has strong ties to the United States. King Abdullah has moved for a free press, democratic reform, and women's rights. King Abdullah's father ruled Jordan through much of its independence. As King Abdullah has moved for even more reforms than his father, both the United States and the European Union have rewarded Jordan with free trade agreements. Jordan is a member of the World Trade Organization. The close ties between Jordan and western nations, coupled with the King and his wife's desire to advance the status of women helped create ExportJordan. ExportJordan was charged with helping to create an entrepreneurial spirit among Jordan's female citizens, and to help them develop and export products. Currently Jordan is successful in exporting clothing, food products, phosphate, and some pharmaceuticals. With the new free trade agreements it was hoped that additional areas could be developed for export.

Trouble from the Start

It was a spirit of adventure and a genuine desire to help others that lead Anne and her husband to Jordan. They were both impressed with the young King and his views for leading his country into the 21st Century. They had hoped to find a cooperative environment, but that hope was somewhat challenged from the start.

When Anne arrived at the offices of ExportJordan for the first time, she met Hayat Maani. Hayat was a western educated young woman with passion. She was deeply concerned with the plight of women in her country and was involved in a number of social causes throughout Jordan. She welcomed Anne and gave her a tour of the offices, explaining what the organization did and what Anne's role would be in the new venture. Anne would work closely with Hayat in helping small businesses owned by Jordanian women to find international buyers for their products. The mission of ExportJordan was to promote all Jordanian products, but Anne would mainly be involved in helping female entrepreneurs. On the initial office tour and series of introduction, Anne met Jafar Faqir, a middle-aged man who worked in the export finance division of the organization. Hayat introduced Jafar to Anne. Jafar did not extend his hand when Anne initiated a handshake and she thought this a bit odd, but quickly forgot about it when Jafar asked her "how do you find Jordan." Anne explained that she had only been in the country a short time but that she was very impressed with the King and his approach to the advancement of women. The look on Jafar's face told Anne that he did not like her response. Hayat told Jafar that Anne would be responsible for promoting women entrepreneurs and Jafar told her to remember these words, "The eye cannot raise above the eyebrow." Hayat shouted to Jafar something in Arabic and Jafar left without saying another word. When Anne asked what had just happened, Hayat simply said that unfortunately not all Jordanian men were supportive of equality for women. Anne would find that this would not be her only negative encounter with Jafar.

The rest of the day went smoothly for Anne as she continued to meet more people associated with the organization. She noticed that all of the women in the offices wore a hejab or headscarf, except for Hayat. Anne noticed other interesting cultural dimensions, such as the common response "Inshallah" or God willing." Many of the people she met seemed very interested in her and asked many questions, such as how many children she and her husband had, especially boys. Anne and her husband had two girls and when she told this to one of her male colleagues, he responded with "Oh, I'm so sorry." Anne knew that it was going to be a very different and interesting experience living in the Middle East.

Progress Begins

Anne and Don settled into their life in Jordan and apart from the normal difficulties of living abroad, the couple didn't feel as if they experienced too much difficulty adjusting. Although there were no other Westerners at ExportJordan, Anne and Don met other American and British expatriates and enjoyed their company and they all enjoyed sharing their experiences living in Jordan. Don kept busy looking for business opportunities for himself and helping Anne with her assignment.

After two months it became clear to Anne that she was in need of an assistant to help her with the preliminary analytical work she was doing. Anne suggested to Hayat that Don be hired to help her. Hayat told her that she didn't think that would be possible, however, she would find someone else to help her. After a few days, Hayat introduced Anne to Karim Dabbas, a young Jordanian man who was hired as her assistant. Karim spoke English well, yet his youth and inexperience gave Anne some concern.

With the help of Karim, Anne completed her initial analysis and was ready to begin to do her fieldwork. Anne had planned on hosting seminars for women around Jordan explaining the possibilities of the export market and finding women with whom she could personally consult about their businesses. Karim would be helpful in the fieldwork, acting as both a driver and interpreter.

The first seminar was planned for Amman and was heavily promoted. Although Anne and Hayat had hoped for a very large audience, they were not unhappy with the few women who attended, because among the attendees were some good prospects for the export market. With Anne's expertise in creating business plans and her knowledge of the U.S. market, Anne and Hayat began helping three women who produced crafts which were felt had international appeal. Additional seminars were planned for other cities in Jordan in the future, and Anne was convinced that she would be able to make a contribution to ExportJordan.

Warnings from Jafar

During the next two weeks Anne and Karim worked with the three women from the seminar on their business plans and creating ways of making their products more appealing to the global marketplace. Anne had not seen Hayat for a few days but she and Karim were busy, and she really didn't need any help from Hayat at that time. One of the female entrepreneurs introduced Anne to two other women who were seeking help with their businesses and so Anne now had five clients to assist. With the increasing workload, Anne began to turn more responsibility over to Karim. Karim was not confident that he could do the work requested by Anne, but she tried to reassure him that he was capable and there would not be any problems.

Karim made slow progress and frequently asked Anne for help with his work. Anne became increasingly frustrated by the slow pace of Karim's work and his constant need for assurances. She developed a nickname for him, "worn sole," meaning that he was wearing out the bottom of his shoes running back and forth from his office to hers asking questions. His nickname appeared appropriate as well to her in that Karim was constantly worried and thus was developing a "worn soul." Karim took the puns in stride but, nevertheless, didn't seem to change his behavior.

One particular incident involving Karim produced difficulties for Anne. She was standing in the hallway talking to another ExportJordan employee when Karim came running down the hall, again looking for her. She mentioned to her coworker "here comes old worn sole again." She continued to tell the coworker about Karim's weaknesses and as she discussed these weaknesses she noticed that Jafar was near and listening. Anne and Jafar did not have much contact with each other, yet the relationship between the two was strained. When they passed in the hall Jafar would not even look at Anne. After once again giving Karim clarification on his task, Anne turned to Jafar and asked him if he needed anything from her. He stared at her for what seemed like a very long time and then muttered, "Just remember this – the family knife does not cut." At this point Anne had had enough with Jafar and his sayings and so she decided to confront him. Jafar turned and went back to his office and Anne followed him. Anne asked Jafar, in a loud voice, "what is it with you and all of these bullshit sayings." Jafar's eyes got big as he pointed his finger towards her and told her that she should be very careful in her "American ways." With no intention of letting this go, Anne sat down in the chair in front of Jafar's desk and propped her feet up on his desk. She told Jafar to sit down, as they needed to talk. Jafar refused to sit down and asked her leave. Anne began to explain to Jafar that she was in Jordan to help the Jordanian people and that by helping women to develop their businesses she was helping all people in Jordan. It appeared to Anne that Jafar was not listening to a word she was saying. After a long silence Anne stood up and walked out of the office. As she was leaving Jafar said to her "Don't you want to know what happened to your friend, Hayat?" When she turned in surprise, Jafar closed and locked the door.

Anne hadn't seen Hayat for a number of days and was curious where she was but now she was concerned. Anne immediately found Karim and asked him if he knew where Hayat was, and he responded that he didn't. He also didn't know if she still worked at ExportJordan. Anne began to ask others in the offices if they knew what happened to Hayat, and it seemed that no one did. One of her colleagues, Mania told her that she thought that Hayat had been fired and that Jafar had something to do with it. Already upset with Jafar, Anne decided that it was time to confront him again. She went to his office and found the door unlocked this time. She barged in and demanded to know what he meant by his statement about Hayat and what happened to her. At first Jafar denied knowing much about the situation and told her that he was only in charge of financing arrangements and that he had no authority over Hayat. Anne losing her temper shouted to Jafar, "Goddamn it Jafar, tell me the truth about Hayat." At that moment it appeared that a calm had come over Jafar. He put his head down and stared at the floor. He then raised his head and told Anne that he wanted her to tell him about "the truth of America's plan to

71

eliminate Palestine." Anne could see that this conversation was not going well and decided just to leave Jafar's office. Before she could go, Jafar approached her, stood very close, and looking into her eyes announced, "Muslim Brotherhood will prevail." Anne felt frightened and threatened as she left the office.

Meeting with the Director

Anne made it straight to her office and felt comfort there. She composed herself and began thinking about what she should do. The organizational structure of ExportJordan was very unstructured and Anne really did not have a supervisor. Hayat acted in some ways as her manager, however, Hayat really did not have formal authority over Anne, and Anne also was not sure whom Jafar reported to as well. Anne decided that perhaps she should schedule an appointment with Dr. Massimi, director of ExportJordan. She felt a bit uncomfortable approaching him directly, but since there really wasn't any formal organizational structure (at least that she knew), she reasoned that it would not be improper. She had met Dr. Massimi on a number of occasions and he appeared to be a very kind and understanding man. She hoped that a meeting with him would clear up what happened to Hayat and resolve the tensions with Jafar.

Anne asked Karim to call and schedule an appointment for her with Dr. Massimi. Karim appeared very nervous and didn't appear to want to talk. He said he would do it as soon as he returned from a meeting. Anne wasn't aware of any meeting involving Karim and he wasn't forthcoming about the details. Anne decided to do some work to get her mind off the Jafar incident. Later in the afternoon Anne came out of her office to check on Karim. He was nowhere to be found. Anne asked if anyone knew where Karim was and was told by one of her colleagues that he was with Jafar. Surprised by this information, Anne went back in her office and decided to call Dr. Massimi herself. Dr. Massimi answered the telephone directly and Anne told him that she needed to see him as soon as possible. He told her that she could come to his office immediately.

Anne entered the office and immediately asked Dr. Massimi what happened to Hayat. Dr. Massimi sat in his chair and without answering, asked her how she was enjoying Jordan. Anne told him that she liked most of the people but that she was having a problem with Jafar. At that moment an assistant brought a tray of tea into the office and offered a cup to Anne. She was too upset to drink tea, she told the assistant. Dr. Massimi took a cup and told Anne to take a cup and that it would calm her. Anne still refused the tea. As Dr. Massimi enjoyed his tea, Anne began to tell him about Jafar. He listened a bit and then asked Anne about her family. Anne told him that they were fine and then preceded to again explain her situation with Jafar. Dr. Massimi listened a bit more and then interrupted Anne again by telling her about his family and told her that his son was studying in the United States. He explained that his son had some difficulties adjusting to American culture. Anne told Dr. Massimi that she and her husband were adjusting well but that she was having problems with her job. Dr. Massimi then began telling a story about his first international job in Iran. He went into great detail about the problems he experienced. Anne listened but wondered if Dr. Massimi was just avoiding her questions.

Anne decided to take another approach. When Dr. Massimi finished his story, Anne told him how happy she was to be able to help Jordanian women and that she was hoping that she could be more successful in her job. Dr. Massimi told her that she was providing a very important service to Jordan and that her work was appreciated. When Anne started to mention Jafar again Dr. Massimi interrupted her to ask if she had visited Petra. When she said that she had planned a visit but had not yet had time, Dr. Massimi began to tell her the history of this ancient city and its importance. Visitors to the office interrupted the history lesson. Three men from the Jordanian Ministry of Tourism stopped by to see Dr. Massimi. He invited them in and introduced them to Anne. Dr. Massimi told the men that he was just talking about Petra and the four men began a discussion about tourist sites in Jordan, and more tea was brought in the office. The four men discussed many things, sometimes in Arabic and sometimes in English, as Anne sat looking at her watch. Getting impatient Anne got up and told Dr. Massimi that she would come back and talk to him "when he could give her his full attention."

Returning to her office, Anne decided that she should compose an email message to Dr. Massimi explaining what she was not able to explain in his office. She explained the situation with Jafar, asked for clarification on Hayat, and told him that she was confused by the structure of the organization.

As Anne was ready to leave for home she checked her email one last time. There was a response from Dr. Massimi. As she anxiously opened the message expecting to get clarification on all the issues, she was shocked to see the response was "Yes, Mrs. Burn, Jordan is a complex country." He did invite her to come to see him again so that they could discuss her situation.

Anne muttered as she turned off her computer "What's the use." She set out for home with the intention of telling her husband that they should look for another opportunity, one not in the Middle East.

SOURCES

Kelly, R. (2003). Countrywatch Jordan Report.
Nydell, M. (2003). Understanding Arabs. Yarmouth, ME: International Press.
www. Countrywatch.com
www.odci/cia/publications/factbook/geos/jo.html
www.state.gov

This case was prepared by Charles A. Rarick.

CASE 9

KIDNAPPED IN COLOMBIA

ABSTRACT

Dan and Melissa Woodruff an American couple moved to Medellin, Colombia, when Dan was offered a position with his company to work with a Colombian partner. Dan was kidnapped by Colombian rebel forces and endures months of captivity as Melissa and others attempted to negotiate his release. Without kidnapping and ransom insurance the negotiation process was difficult and ended very badly.

Although Melissa Woodruff still felt compassion for the people of Colombia, she now realized that she made the biggest mistake of her life when she encouraged her husband to accept a temporary assignment in Medellin. As she reflected on that decision, she felt as if she would never recover from the Colombian experience.

An International Opportunity

Melissa and Dan Woodruff met in college and married as soon as Dan graduated. Although the couple wanted to start a family, they decided that it would be best to wait until Dan became more established in his career as a marketing manager with Carolina Textiles. The couple settled into a nice home in South Carolina and Melissa was able to complete her undergraduate degree in fashion merchandising. Melissa wanted to design women's clothing, but she had difficulty securing a position with an established company. She instead began to design and manufacture her own line and sold the garments on eBay. Although she didn't make much money, she greatly enjoyed the challenge of designing a piece of clothing and seeing its actual completion. Dan did well in his career at Carolina Textiles and the couple thought that they might spend their entire lives in the tranquil surroundings of the small South Carolina town where Carolina Textiles was headquartered. However, that vision was not to be.

After working for Carolina Textiles for only five years, Dan was offered an opportunity that he never envisioned. The firm offered Dan the opportunity to manage a large manufacturing arrangement, which the firm had recently established in Colombia. In an effort to reduce labor costs, Carolina Textiles had contracted with a local textile manufacturer in Medellin, and the company needed someone to manage the day-to-day operations, and to protect Carolina Textiles interests in Colombia. Colombia was seen as one of the desirable locations for foreign manufacturing in that Colombia, along with Bolivia, Peru, and Ecuador were part of the Andean Trade Preferences Act. The Act was amended in 2003, which provided for textiles to be brought into the United States, duty-free, provided that the products were manufactured with U.S. cloth. The city of Medellin seemed like a good choice in that the city had a long history in textile manufacturing. Many of the local manufacturing facilities in Medellin operate in free trade zones, or "Plan Vallejo," and they export much of their output to the United States. The industry was well developed and accustomed to exporting.

Dan, and especially Melissa were at first hesitant about spending two to three years in Colombia. Not only would they miss their friends in South Carolina, but they were aware of the political violence in Colombia. After a visit to Medellin, and after much discussion, the couple decided to give it a try. Melissa reasoned that the experience would be good for Dan's career, and he would be getting a promotion along with the assignment. The couple was still young and could start a family after the assignment. The fact that the couple could easily afford to have a maid who would also cook for them was appealing. Melissa also felt that she could continue her design business, and perhaps, even expand it with the abundant manufacturing facilities in Medellin. The couple sold their home in South Carolina, said good-bye to friends, and headed for the challenges that awaited them in Colombia.

Life in Colombia

Dan and Melissa settled into a rented three-bedroom home in the suburbs of Medellin. For the most part the couple enjoyed living in the "City of Eternal Spring," however; life in Medellin was also stressful. Without much international travel experience, and only a very basic proficiency in Spanish, the couple experienced a significant degree of culture shock.

Melissa would email friends about how different it was living in Colombia; from seeing all the armed guards at the mall, to the ability to purchase medicine at a pharmacy without a prescription. Everyday presented its own set of challenges for Dan and Melissa but the couple adjusted fairly well. Dan was busy with work and Melissa was scouting out new ways to establish her design business.

Dan and Melissa had been warned about the political troubles and violence in Colombia. Before leaving the United States they read much on the history of Colombia. They were especially interested in the revolutionary groups that operated against the government. Dan and Melissa learned that Colombia was still a divided country with the smaller, but dominate population of European descent often in conflict with the larger population of mixed ethnicity. The two rival political groups which developed in Colombia, the Conservatives and Liberals had fought in a bloody civil war called "La Violencia" which began in 1948. The main revolutionary group, the Revolutionary Armed Forces of Colombia or FARC developed out of the frustration of some members of the Liberal party. In the 1980s FARC began to fund its revolutionary cause by taxing the illegal drug industry of Colombia. The group continued to control an increasingly larger share of the country and now claims over 40% of Colombia. FARC also began to diversify its source of funding through the kidnapping of prominent Colombians and expatriates. While the kidnapping threat worried Dan and Melissa, they reasoned that neither one of them was a likely target for kidnapping since they were "just average people." They did not limit their outings and generally tried to blend into Colombian society including frequent attendance at the bullfighting events in the city.

The couple felt acclimated to the culture, for the most part, after about six months. Melissa enjoyed getting dressed up and shopping. She enjoyed buying gifts to send back home to friends. The couple developed a daily routine in which Dan would leave for work every weekday morning at 8:30 A.M. driving himself, and Melissa would begin her day on the Internet, answering emails and developing business ideas. Although the couple did not have the opportunity to make many American friends, they did enjoy the company of a few Colombian couples from Dan's work. Melissa truly enjoyed these friendships and developed a degree of sympathy for the less fortunate members of Medellin society. Sometimes she would open her wallet and drop a large cash roll (large by Colombian standards) into the hat or canister of street beggars. This made her feel as if she was making a big difference in someone's life, something she felt she could not do in the United States.

The compassion she felt towards the Colombian people was not tempered even when her purse was snatched in the local market. While she had the equivalent of about $200 U.S. in the purse, she was more concerned about replacing her credit cards and identification. This made shopping difficult in that she would have to carry cash for all transactions, including larger transactions. The purse snatching worried Dan, but he reassured himself that petty crime was a problem in Colombia and that the couple would just have to be more careful. The event passed quickly, and was almost forgotten when a very impressive article was written in the local newspaper profiling Dan and Carolina Textiles. The article was clipped and mailed back to a number of friends in the United States. The couple felt as if they were making new friends in Colombia and that Dan's career was heading in a very positive direction.

Taken Hostage

All of this, however, was about to change. On a particularly spring-like day, as Dan left for work he had much on his mind. There were a number of improvements he hoped to suggest to the contract manufacturer, including the addition of a more efficient computerized layout pattern for cutting cloth. As he drove the usual route to his office he was reviewing the different supplier options for the new software, and he kept thinking about the recent article about himself in the newspaper. Suddenly his thoughts were interrupted as the vehicle in front of him came to a stop and the driver opened the hood of the car. A second vehicle moved very and very closely behind Dan's new 700 series BMW, so close in fact that Dan was concerned that the two vehicles would crash. Dan motioned to the driver of the van behind him to move back. Instead four armed men wearing handkerchiefs over their noses and mouths got out of the van, grabbed Dan, and placed a cloth sack over his head. They pushed him into the back of the van and quickly took off. Dan, unable to see what was happening, and unable to understand much of what was being said was confused and scared. Surely he thought to himself, "I'm not being kidnapped. They must have made a mistake." Unable to see, and having some difficulty breathing Dan tried to speak to his captors in English, but he got no response. Dan kept asking them "what's going on" and trying to assure them that they must be making a mistake. After a few hours of riding in the back of the hot van and having no water, Dan was hopeful when the van stopped and the door opened. He hoped the ordeal was coming to an end. Unfortunately for Dan, the ordeal was just beginning. He was placed inside another vehicle and it was the beginning of a very long drive into the remote areas of Colombia - an area Dan and Melissa had planned on visiting some day, although under very different circumstances.

Back at home, Melissa was very busy planning her day when someone knocked at the door. Adriana, the housekeeper answered the door as usual and came very quickly calling for Senora Woodruff. She said a man had left this note for her and she seemed very upset. Melissa was confused as she opened the paper she had been given. The note, written in broken English, stated that her husband had been kidnapped and that she should get a short-wave radio. The note indicated a frequency to use with the radio and the times to use it. It was signed "Gabino." Melissa asked Adriana what this all meant and she told her that Senor Woodruff had been taken by FARC and that he was in great danger. Melissa was beginning to become very upset, however, she retained her composure and called Dan's office, hoping it wasn't true. When Dan's assistant told her that he had not yet arrived, she immediately called his mobile phone. There was no answer. Melissa was now frantic. She called Dan's assistant again and explained what had happened. The assistant, Manuel Chacon told her to stay calm and that he would immediately come to the house. Melissa asked Adriana if she should call the police and Adriana told her that it would not be advisable.

When Manuel arrived he told Melissa to remain calm. He had already contacted Carolina Textiles and told them what had happened. Manuel told Melissa that, unfortunately, kidnapping of foreigners was common in Colombia, but that Dan would be released as soon as Carolina Textiles paid the ransom that would be demanded by FARC. Manuel assured Melissa that no harm would come to Dan and that he would be released very soon. Manuel told Melissa that there was nothing that they could do at this time but purchase the short-wave radio and wait for the designated time to contact the kidnappers. He also advised her to pray for a safe and quick return of her husband. Melissa decided to call her parents whom she had little contact with since moving against their wishes to Colombia. It would be a difficult call but she needed their support.

In quick time Manuel purchased the short-wave radio and set it up in the Woodruff's home. He was in constant contact with Carolina Textiles and he relayed their concern to Melissa. Manuel also had to report to Melissa that Carolina Textiles did not have ransom insurance and that this made the situation more difficult. He reassured Melissa that once the kidnappers learned of this fact they would release Dan, maybe with a "token ransom payment." Melissa, after contacting her parents got their pledge to help pay the ransom.

Negotiations Begin

Three very long days passed before Melissa and Manuel were able to make contact with Gabino, the FARC negotiator. Manuel explained how Dan was not a wealthy man and that the company he worked for did not carry ransom insurance. Gabino told Manuel that unless a $2,000,000 US ransom was paid for Dan they would never see him alive again. Manuel again insisted that this was not possible, however, Gabino was unsympathic. The first contact ended without any hope of agreement. Manuel was instructed to try again, once he had arranged for the money transfer. Manuel assured Melissa that the demands were just typical bargaining and that if she could raise about $50,000 US the matter could be settled. Melissa knew that she could raise that much with their savings and the help of her parents. Dan's parents were deceased. Manuel told Melissa that he would seek the help of Carolina Textiles.

With the help of Manuel, Carolina Textiles decided that they should contact a kidnapping and ransom expert to help with the negotiations. Since they did not carry kidnapping and ransom insurance they would have to pay the costs of the negotiator but it was felt that this was a small price to pay for their employee's safety. The external negotiator would not arrive in Medellin for three days, enough time for Manuel to try again with Gabino. On the second attempt at negotiation the same situation arose. Manuel told the kidnappers that they should release Dan since he was not able to pay the ransom and Gabino continued to make threats. Manuel offered the $50,000 with an expectation that the negotiators would agree to a quick resolution. Gabino told Manuel, with Melissa listening, that for $50,000 he would cut off a certain body part from Dan and mail it to Dan's wife. Melissa became frantic and the second session ended very badly.

During all this time, Dan was still traveling with his captors deeper into the Colombian jungle. The first few days he was riding in several vehicles but afterwards he was on foot, always chained to his captors. Dan tried repeatedly to explain that he was not an important person and that no sizable ransom could be paid. He truly believed that the captors would release him, even if in the middle of a jungle, once they believed their effort would not result in a ransom. Although Dan was optimistic that he would be released, he felt very helpless and vulnerable. He worried how Melissa would be handling the news of his abduction. Although exhausted and poorly fed, Dan continued to insist that he be released. Each day brought increasing frustration for Dan, and Melissa.

Melissa began searching the Internet for information about kidnapping. She learned that on an average day 10 people are kidnapped in Colombia. She also learned that in most cases the kidnappers would eventually settle for 10-20% of the original demands. The prospects for a safe return of the hostage were not very good if the negotiation was not conducted properly. Further searching revealed that many companies, which operate in countries with a high probability of kidnapping, carry kidnapping and ransom (K&R) insurance. The policies typically cover the ransom payment, consultant fees, and transportation needed to deliver the ransom and return of the hostage. It appeared that many companies which carry K&R insurance do not advertise the fact for fear that their employees will more likely become targets of kidnapping. Melissa began to wonder if Carolina Textiles did in fact have K&R insurance but it was not being disclosed at this time.

The Security Consultant

Melissa heard a knock at the door and a man entered. It was Charles Griffith, a security consultant hired by Carolina Textile to help negotiate the release of Dan Charles introduced himself and appeared to have great confidence in his abilities. He told Melissa not to worry, and that he had successfully handled the negotiations for two other expatriates one in Mexico and one in Venezuela. He did state that because Carolina Textiles had no K&R insurance it would make the negotiations more difficult. Melissa told Charles that she had read on the Internet that the typical settlement was between 10-20% of the initial demand and that she could probably raise that amount with the help of the company. Charles just responded by saying "we will see."

Charles began the negotiation process with Gabino and the first session did not go well. Gabino at first refused to talk to him and asked to speak with Manuel. Charles informed him that he, Charles, would be handling the negotiations from now on. The communication ended when Charles asked for proof that the rebels did in fact have Dan and that he was alive. Melissa began to worry that Charles was not the right choice for the negotiation sessions and confided this to Manuel.

Days went by and there was no response from Gabino. Feeling

frustrated, Melissa asked Manuel to once again attempt to contact Gabino. He agreed and they decided that they would tell Charles that he should defer to Manuel, at least for a while. Charles strongly opposed this suggestion but agreed to let Manuel do the next session due to the strong insistence of Melissa. He encouraged Manuel to explain that a new negotiator was working for the family.

For Dan, boredom was becoming a major issue. He spent his days at a rebel camp, chained either to a tree or to his bed. Dan would often think of Melissa and the various trips they took together back in the United States. He sometimes replayed movies he had seen in his head to relieve the boredom. The heat, lack of food and water, and constant boredom were beginning to fray his nerves. His frequent outburst caused some guerrillas to threaten him with death. All the rebels carried assault rifles and machetes, and some of them appeared to enjoy the possibility of doing harm to Dan. On a couple of occasions Dan attempted to befriend some of the younger rebels by explaining, in broken Spanish, that he and his company were trying to help the Colombian people by creating jobs. It didn't seem that this mattered to the rebels.

Back in Medellin, with Manuel again doing the negotiations it appeared that progress was being made. Gabino told Manuel that it might be possible to release Dan if $1,500,000 could be paid quickly. While it was impossible for Melissa to raise that much money, even with the offer of $100,000 from Carolina Textiles, at least the kidnapper's demands were being reduced. Manuel also was able to have proof delivered, via a photo of Dan holding a copy of El Tiempo (a daily Colombian newspaper) and he seemed to be developing some rapport with Gabino. Charles, while listening to the negotiations offered suggestions to Manuel, but he was becoming increasingly dissatisfied with the role he was playing.

Charles reported back to Carolina Textiles and expressed his concerns with the fact that Melissa was insisting on having Manuel do the negotiating. Charles expressed his doubts that Manuel could ever reach a settlement. The CEO of Carolina Textiles, Ben Goodin called Melissa to persuade her to allow Charles to take over the negotiations. Melissa insisted that Manuel was better suited for the negotiations and that the life of her husband was at stake. Mr. Goodin was not about to press the issue further, and so he wished Melissa luck and asked that he be kept informed. When news got back to Charles that he was not going to be doing the negotiations he decided to leave Colombia. He did offer suggestions to Manuel and told both Manuel and Melissa that the process could take some time.

Every third day Manuel attempted to contact Gabino. Most of the time there was only static over the airways. The process continued for five long months and it was clear that Melissa was feeling the strain. While Carolina Textiles continued to pay Dan's salary, Melissa felt as if they could do more. Not much progress was being made, however, Gabino did agree to reduce the ransom to $1,000,000. This amount was still much more than Melissa could raise. It appeared to her that time was running out and that there was little hope of rescuing Dan.

A Sign of Hope

It was during one of the darkest periods when a bright spot developed for Melissa. A reporter from the BBC was doing a story on Colombian kidnappings and he interviewed her for the story. Once the article was published, Carolina Textiles developed an increased interest in Dan's safety. Mr. Goodin told Melissa that the company was prepared to help with the ransom to the tune of $250,000 and that he would be sending yet another security expert down to Colombia to help in the negotiations. Melissa felt that the $250,000 may be enough for the rebels, and she could even add more from their savings and the contributions from her parents, if needed. Mr. Goodin insisted that the new security expert would be making the new offers and that he would be more successful than Manuel had been.

Upon hearing the good news, Manuel and Melissa contacted Gabino and told him that the company was prepared to make a final offer of $250,000 and that a new negotiator would be contacting him to arrange for the transfer of funds and delivery of the hostage. Gabino did not share the excitement of Manuel and Melissa and all he said to them was that the amount was "not sufficient." Although somewhat surprised by the reaction, Melissa and Manuel maintained their optimism and awaited the arrival of the new negotiator.

Melissa and Manuel met the new security expert at the airport. Frederick Hervitz was a very experienced hostage negotiator and he wasted no time in telling Manuel and Melissa what they would be doing. Frederick insisted that he, and he alone, would be talking to Gabino. Melissa felt confident in Frederick's abilities and was optimistic that the ordeal would soon be over. Manuel agreed that Frederick should take over the negotiations. He was impressed with Frederick and besides; the whole process was becoming a strain on him personally. Manuel and Melissa told Frederick what they had done and what they had accomplished. He told them that they had made many mistakes.

Bringing Dan Home

Frederick attempted many times to reach Gabino, but each time all he heard was static. Frederick at first assumed that Gabino was just making it difficult on him in order to raise the ransom, and lower the expectations of Melissa and the company; however, the long silence did begin to worry Frederick. Weeks went by and there was no communication with Gabino. Mr. Goodin telephoned Melissa and told her not to worry, that Frederick would be bringing Dan home soon.

The words of Mr. Goodin were all too true. After six months of enduring the ordeal, Melissa received a call from the American embassy in Bogotá. It was bad news. Melissa was informed that a body, that appeared to be her husband had been discovered in a remote northern province of Colombia. Melissa was devastated. She couldn't speak. She thought, surely it is a mistake, but deep down she feared it was true. Frederick arranged a flight to Bogotá for Melissa, Manuel, and himself. Melissa positively identified the body, although Dan looked much different to her than the last time she saw him. He was dirty, had a long beard, and he looked much older. The cause of death was not readily apparent. It deeply saddened Melissa that the last days of Dan's life were spent in such dire conditions.

As Melissa prepared to take the body of her dead husband back to the United States for burial, she couldn't help wonder what went wrong and why the negotiations were unsuccessful. She loved the Colombian people she had met, and she hated the country. Melissa deeply regretted the decision to become an expatriate in Colombia.

SOURCES

DuBois, J. (1994). Cultures of the World: Colombia. New York: Marshall Cavendish.

McDermott, J. (2002). *Colombia's Most Powerful Rebels*. BBC News. January 7.

McDermott, J. (2002). *Analysis: Colombia's Security Crisis*. BBC News. May 4.

www.countrywatch.com/colombia. Accessed on July 22, 2003.

This case was prepared by Charles A. Rarick.

EXERCISE 5

CULTURAL FILTERS IN PERCEPTION

Purpose: The purpose of this exercise is to generate a discussion on the influence of culture on one's perception and communication.

Procedure: Read the paragraph below and count the number of times the letter "F" appears in the paragraph. Write the number of F's down.

The instructor will only allow 20 seconds for you to read the paragraph and write down your answer.

Paragraph: FINAL FOOTAGE OF THE FILM CAME FROM THE COPY OF THE MASTER PRODUCTION AND OF THE ADDITIONAL FILM RESERVES FOUND IN THE ARCHIVES.

EXERCISE 6

CROSS-CULTURAL NEGOTIATIONS

Purpose: The purpose of this exercise is to develop more familiarity and skill in assessing the impact of culture on the negotiation process.

Procedure: Read the background notes that follow and then assemble into two negotiating teams. Your instructor will assign your team to either the Alpha or Beta culture. The exercise works best if team members only read the cultural characteristics of their assigned culture. In other words, if you are assigned to the Alpha culture, only read the Alpha segment that follows. If you are assigned to the Beta culture, only read the Beta segment that follows. Each team will have 3-5 members that conduct the actual negotiations, and additional members can be present, acting as observers.

Background Note:

A company from Alpha, is visiting Beta, in order to discuss the possibilities of arranging a contract to manufacture shoes. The Alpha company wants to find a low cost, yet reliable source of production. The Beta company is in a country with inexpensive labor and is interested in gaining the manufacturing contract. The purpose of the meeting today is to see if a contract can be negotiated between the two parties. The negotiations should result in an agreement concerning basic issues such as price per shoe, quality assurances, and delivery, and any additional items either team decides is important. Each team will have a chief negotiator and two or three assistants.

Alpha Culture

The Alpha company consists of negotiators from a culture which possesses the ollowing characteristics:

> high power distance
> masculine
> individualistic
> high uncertainty avoidance
> low context

Your team will be very aggressive in seeking a shoe price of less than $5 per unit and may suggest methods of increasing efficiency in order to achieve that low price.

Beta Culture

The Beta company consists of negotiators from a culture which possesses the following characteristics:

> low power distance
> feminine
> collectivist
> low uncertainty avoidance
> high context

Your team is willing to manufacture each shoe for no less than $8 per unit. While labor costs are generally low in your country, many benefits must be paid to workers which increases the cost of each worker.

PART THREE

GLOBAL ALLIANCES, STRATEGY, AND LOCATION DECISIONS

Motivation for firms to internationalize their operations include the pursuit of new market opportunities and less expensive and/or better inputs. Firms can internationalize through various ways such as exporting, joint ventures, strategic alliances, and new wholly-owned subsidiaries. However, firms that internationalize might encounter geographical, cultural, political, and economic differences associated with new host countries. Consequently, firms might encounter new management problems such as managing cultural diversity and dealing with host governments. International firms face cultural diversity in term of religion, values, education, and social structure. The following cases provide some examples of business risks and management problems facing several firms during their international establishment and operations.

Cases:
Tiger Surgical Supplies
SPB International's Plant Location Decision
Red Dragon Enterprises

Exercises:
Comparative Strategy

CASE 10

TIGER SURGICAL SUPPLIES, LTD

Pouncing on Doi Moi Opportunities in the Emerging Economy of Vietnam

ABSTRACT

With the liberalization of economy in 1987, foreign direct investment (FDI) began to flow into Vietnam. This paper presents a case study of a French manufacturer of surgical supplies who establishes a production facility near Ho Chi Minh City in an attempt to capitalize on Vietnam's low labor costs. The case explores the difficulties the company experiences in its dealings with the Vietnamese government, and a variety of cross-cultural management issues are addressed as well. The focus of the case is a French expatriate and a Vietnamese repatriate who experience many unforeseen difficulties in establishing and operating a facility in this newly emerging economy.

Bordeaux Plastique Fabriquant, S.A., a French surgical supply company decided in 1994 to establish a production facility in Ho Chi Minh City, Vietnam. The company selected Vietnam as the sight for increased production capacity due to very low labor costs, and the possibility of exporting to Southeast Asian countries. Management of Bordeaux felt that Vietnamese workers would be very motivated and that labor problems would be nonexistent. Bordeaux also concluded that due to Vietnam's desire to attract foreign capital, establishing a foreign subsidiary in this newly emerging economy would be easy and government relations with the company would be good. Unfortunately for Bordeaux, none of these assumptions would prove to be correct.

Vietnam

Located in South East Asia, Vietnam has attracted the attention of Western governments since at least the 19th Century. In 1858 the French colonized Vietnam. After internal fighting in an eight-year war, the French signed the Geneva Agreement in 1954 that lead to their withdrawal from the country and the division of Vietnam into the communist north and noncommunist south. The Geneva Agreement required elections to be held for unification, however, the government in the south refused the elections and proclaimed itself the Republic of Vietnam. During the late 1950's conflict escalated between the north and south that led President Kennedy to send U.S. military advisors to Vietnam in 1961. In 1965 President Johnson sent military combat forces to Vietnam. The war in Vietnam escalated, and without a clear sign of victory the American public grew tired of the conflict. In 1973 a peace agreement was reached and the U.S. withdrew its military forces from Vietnam. Within two years the communist government from the north invaded the south and unified the country into the Socialist Republic of Vietnam.

With its socialist economic system suffering, Vietnam instituted economic reforms in 1986 referred to a doi moi, indicating that the country was ready to move towards a market economy. With the liberalization of the economy, Vietnam began to experience rapid economic growth. Many Western companies raced into Vietnam due to its low labor costs and the belief that Vietnam was an untapped market. Although the government of Vietnam is still communist, the economy has become more capitalistic. The government, however, still maintains significant control over the economy and operates many state-owned enterprises. Government bureaucracy and corruption are often seen as impediments to further economic growth.

Early Difficulties with the Government

Philippe Desmarest, a ten-year veteran of Bordeaux was placed in charge of all governmental relations for the proposed joint venture. If successful, Philippe would become the chief operating officer of the new facility. Because he had successfully negotiated an international joint venture agreement with Mexican authorities a few years prior to this assignment, Philippe was considered by management to be the best candidate to negotiate with the Vietnamese. . Philippe made several trips to Hanoi to meet with governmental officials, including officials at the Ministry of Planning and Investment (MPI). He knew that it was critical that MPI officials agree to any foreign investment project so he was always well prepared for his meetings. Philippe prepared many reports that showed how a proposed joint venture between Bordeaux and a local partner would benefit Vietnam. Philippe was proposing that Bordeaux and its Vietnamese partner establish a joint venture called Tiger Surgical Supplies (TSS) and that the company produce surgical gloves, protective goggles, and fluid resistant gowns for export to Europe and Asia. If initial production were successful, Tiger would then expand production into other surgical supply areas.

While Philippe was assured by his Vietnamese consultants, and by the joint venture partner, that Vietnam was very open to foreign investment, the meetings with the Vietnamese government did not always go smoothly. It appeared to Philippe that the government officials were often confused by what he was proposing, and that they also had some suspicions about the intentions of his company. When negotiations dragged on for months, Philippe became discouraged and decided to recommend to the top management of Bordeaux that the company begin looking for another country in which to locate the plant. When word of this action reached governmental officials at the Ministry of Planning and Investment, the necessary permits for the plant were approved immediately. Philippe decided that a tough approach in dealing with the Vietnamese was the most effective strategy.

A Slow Start

Tiger Surgical Supply had purchased a building that was previously a state-owned enterprise. The facilities were in need of much repair, but Philippe felt that with the abundance of extremely low labor costs in Vietnam the building could be brought up to the necessary standards in a short time, and with little expense. After much more time than expected, and at a much greater expense than anticipated, Tiger Surgical Supply was ready for production in the spring of 1997. While the Vietnamese partner had helped with some governmental and construction contacts, the partner's role in the venture was practically nonexistent. Philippe preferred this passive association.

Philippe had selected Nguyen Tam Chien (a French citizen who left Vietnam as a child) to be the founding plant manager for the new joint venture. He had been educated in France and Belgium in economics, business administration, and management and spoke passable Vietnamese. In Vietnam, Chien was called a "Viet Kieu" or "overseas Vietnamese." He belonged to a large group of Vietnamese who fled the country after the fall of Saigon fearing life under a communist government. Chien's family first settled in the United States, but after a brief stay, relocated to France. Chien was now very interested in helping his former country achieve economic gains, and he welcomed the opportunity to help start a new business venture in the country. Although returning to Vietnam was a hardship, Chien felt a sense of responsibility to his former homeland.

Both Philippe and Chien were surprised by the number of applications that were submitted in response to the advertisement for production positions. Many of the applicants were well educated, and it became difficult to select the few needed from the large mass of applications. Philippe delegated responsibility for employee selection to Chien, and with the help of his assistant, Pham Hi Thi, the two selected what they considered to be the best candidates. One of the criteria for selection was the lack of production experience. Chien felt that if he selected employees with previous experience in production that they would bring the bad habits that they learned under state controlled operations to TSS. He wanted to be able to train the new employees in Western work methods.

Production got off to a slow start, and lagged far behind initial expectations. Philippe reasoned that it would take some time for the employees to gain an appreciation for new concepts like productivity and efficiency. Chien was not as patient and was constantly complaining to Thi about the lack of motivation he found among the workers. Chien, who was from what was formerly South Vietnam, blamed the communists for ruining the work ethic of the Vietnamese people. One of the habits that Chien found especially hard to accept was the practice of napping in the afternoon. Chien would find that at times the entire production process would be silent and everyone in the factory would be resting or napping for about an hour. Thi explained to Chien that it was customary in Vietnam to allow an afternoon nap. Although Chien did not see the reason for this practice, he relented with the understanding that employees would not be paid for the time they spent not working.

Relations between Chien and many of the workers did not appear to be good. It was obvious to all that Chien often became frustrated with the workers and would openly express his disapproval. It appeared to Philippe that many of the workers did not appear to like Chien, and he wasn't sure why. Chien was a very dedicated, conscientious, and serious manager, and he had made a personal sacrifice to return to Vietnam to help his former country. He expected much from his employees; however, he had a soft side as well and a true desire to make Vietnam a more prosperous country. Philippe thought that some of the ill will between Chien and the work force came from Chien's early effort to fire some poor performing employees. Chien had selected 16 employees who consistently performed poorly and gave them one week to improve. Thi cautioned Chien on this move, however, Chien insisted. Without exception all the targeted employees showed no improvement and it was decided that all 16 employees would be fired. It was with great surprise that Chien learned that terminating employment in Vietnam was no simple matter, and that the workers could appeal the decision to the People's Committee, which they did. The People's Committee reinstated all the employees, much to the displeasure of Chien.

While it was intended that TSS would be staffed by as many locals as possible, Philippe felt that there might be a need for additional expatriates to manage the operation. He considered recruiting managers from Thailand who could help bring a more "business" perspective to the supervision of TSS employees. Chien and Thi disagreed and convinced Philippe that it was important that the management of TSS be "homegrown" in order to gain favor with the Vietnamese government and to help develop a managerial class in Vietnam. Furthermore, they argued, having Vietnamese supervisors would provide incentive for operational level employees to work hard in the hope of gaining an internal promotion. While Philippe finally agreed, he worried that most Vietnamese had been trained in management under the communist system and that it was a very ineffective way of running an organization. He feared that France would soon begin to put pressure on him to improve operations.

Tigers, Horses, Monkeys

With an urgent need for organizational efficiency, Philippe decided that TSS needed an incentive plan to increase worker motivation. He instructed Chien to develop a plan that he thought would work. Chien consulted Thi, who recommended against radical change, and recommended instead that wages be based on a piece-rate system. Chien thought that a more systematic approach was needed, and developed a program to revamp the organizational structure. Feeling that it was not practical to attempt to fire more workers, Chien created three different classes of employees. The highest class, the Tiger class would be paid the highest salary and be the only employees eligible for promotion. Tigers would wear red clothing and be given more privileges than the other classes of workers. The second-class employees, the Horses would be paid less than the Tigers, but more than the lowest class of employees, the Monkeys. The Horses would wear black clothing and be eligible for certain limited benefits. The

Horse class was seen as average performers who, if they improved, could be placed in the highest class. The poorest performing employees would be placed in the Monkey class and would not be eligible for promotion or overtime assignments, nor any special benefits such as company sponsored dinners and entertainment. Monkeys would wear brown clothing and were expected to pay respect to all employees in the higher classes. Being in the lowest class was intended to punish and humiliate employees who were placed in that class. While the two lowest classes could advance, a general feeling existed that the Monkeys would never be able to move from their position. Philippe noticed that class membership tended to correlate with age, and that the Tigers were generally a younger group of employees. It was hoped that the very visible class structure would motivate employees to either improve or quit the company. The strong desire to save face would be a strong motivator, or so thought Chien.

The employees, many of whom refused to wear the appropriate uniforms, immediately challenged the class system of employment. A particularly unpleasant event occurred shortly after the plan was announced. The body of a dead monkey was placed over the opening of the plant gate, wearing a brown shirt, and its face covered with an image resembling that of Chien. Continued tensions existed with the class system, and eventually it deteriorated to the point that the only differences among group members were pay and benefits. The system, with all its problems did; however, appear to raise overall efficiency of the operation. The Tigers who operated in teams were very productive, and many of the Horses were showing signs of improvement. The employees classified as Monkeys continued to perform poorly.

Expansion Plans

With some of the initial problems resolved, Philippe was eager to expand production into other areas. The current facility could be expanded and additional workers hired to capitalize on the increased concern over the spreading of the AIDS virus in Asia and the subsequent increase in sales of prophylactics. While Bordeaux did not manufacturer prophylactics, Philippe felt that TSS was in a good position to expand the product line for the company. He suggested to his managers at Bordeaux that they consider expanding the production capacity of TSS. Bordeaux authorized a feasibility study of the market, and the report indicated that a low cost provider could gain a competitive advantage in the Southeast Asian market. With the favorable report Philippe was given the authority to begin expansion plans for TSS.

Following the same course that he had followed in the initial approach to establishing the joint venture, Philippe contacted the Vietnamese government officials in Hanoi and informed them of the expansion plans. He felt that the officials would be delighted that TSS was increasing its investment in Vietnam and that the company would be increasing its employment. The Vietnamese officials, however, who appeared uninterested in the expansion plans, did not match his enthusiasm. Philippe was told that he would have to contact Tran Hung, a MPI official in Ho Chi Minh City who he was told may approve the expansion. Hung told Philippe that he had some concerns about the expansion of TSS. Through a translator he told Philippe that it seemed that TSS was "too French" and that the Vietnamese joint venture partner was exercising not enough influence. He recommended that Philippe consider an additional Vietnamese partner, maybe someone in government who could help him with the necessary connections that he would need to expand his facility. It was obvious to Philippe that Hung was suggesting that he be included in the investment. This was completely unacceptable to Philippe, and so he decided to consult Chien and Thi concerning his options.

Chien felt that TSS should reject any involvement of government officials in the joint venture, and that Philippe should return to MPI and demand that the expansion plans be approved. Thi did not appear to agree with Chien, but she remained mostly silent. Chien reasoned that after all, it was the threat of withholding investment which was successful in securing the initial permits for the plant. Given the advice offered by Chien Philippe scheduled another appointment with Hung. On his arrival, Philippe was greeted with warm enthusiasm by Hung. Philippe thought that someone in a superior position to Hung must have instructed him to be more cooperative in matter of foreign investment. So it came as a great surprise to Philippe that Hung's mood shifted dramatically when he was informed by Philippe that no government official would be involved in TSS, and that TSS expected the permission for expansion to be approved as soon as possible. Hung was noticeably upset and informed Philippe that he may be making a big mistake. Philippe informed Hung that the decision was final, and in a loud voice warned Hung that it was he who may be making a big mistake. Philippe threatened Hung with adverse action from his superiors in Hanoi if he didn't do his part to gain approval for expansion. As Philippe left the office he looked back at Hung who was smoking a cigarette at his desk and smiling.

Cutting the Tall Poppy

The following day began with some troubling news from the port from which TSS shipped its products for export. A delivery driver for TSS was phoning to tell Chien that the customs inspectors were not allowing any TSS product to be loaded for shipment. The driver refused to give a reason, and seemed to be confused as to why the action was being taken. Philippe immediately thought of Hung and proceeded to go to his office and confront him about the actions of the customs inspectors. Upon arriving at Hung's office Philippe was informed that Hung was unavailable for the rest of the day. After three days had passed Philippe was finally able to schedule an appointment with Hung. Frustrated by the delay in seeing Hung, and frustrated by customs problems, Philippe in an angry manner accused Hung of interfering with the export shipments. Using a translator Hung denied any involvement. He did tell Philippe that he had heard that the customs inspectors were concerned about possible black market products leaving the country in TSS containers. Hung told Philippe that he could help him with the problem, and that it would only require the payment of an "inspection fee" of two dollars a container. Philippe felt that he had no choice but to agree to the fee since all of TSS's exports were pilling up on the loading docks. He told Hung that the inspection fee would be paid, and that he needed Hung to instruct the customs agents to immediately clear the goods for shipment. Philippe returned to his office feeling exploited by the whole experience. His feelings of exploitation were increased when word came from the docks that the goods were still not being loaded. Philippe immediately called Hung who informed him that now the loaders were demanding a loading fee of one dollar a container. Philippe remain silent for a moment and then asked Hung why TSS was being singled out for these additional fees. Hung paused for a moment and then replied in English that "the tall poppies get cut first." Not sure what he was implying, Philippe told Hung that TSS would pay the additional dollar fee to the loaders. It was at this point that Philippe was questioning his decision to promote Vietnam as a desirable location for a production facility. While the additional fees were small, Philippe didn't like the idea of paying what essentially amounted to a bribe, and he wondered what else Hung had in mind to punish him for not agreeing to include him in the partnership expansion plans. Philippe wondered if the government would ever approve the expansion, and if he had made a mistake in recommending Vietnam as an investment location.

SOURCES

Buchel, B. and T. Lai Xuan. (2001). *Measures of Joint Venture Performance from Multiple Perspectives: An Evaluation of Local and Foreign Managers in Vietnam.* Asian Pacific Journal of Management, 18(1), 101-111.

Curry, J. and C. Nguyen. (1997). Passport Vietnam. San Rafael, CA: World Trade Press.

Prasso, S. (1999). *Vietnam: Welcome Back?* Business Week. August, 16.

Triandis, H., Carnevale, P., Gelfand, M., Robert, C., Wasti, D., Chen, X., Kim, U., Dreu, C., Vliert, E., Iwao, S., Ohbuchi, K., and P. Schmitz. (2001). *Culture and Deception in Business Negotiations: A Multilevel Analysis.* International Journal of Cross Cultural Management, 1(1), 73-90.

Venard, B. (1998). *Vietnam in Mutation: Will it be the Next Tiger or a Future Jaguar?* Asian pacific Journal of Management, 15(1), 77-95.

Webster, L. (1999). *The New Breed.* Vietnam Business Journal, 8(4), 1-8.

www.state.gov/backgroundnotes/Vietnam. Accessed on June 8, 2002.

This case was prepared by Charles A. Rarick and previously published in the Proceedings of Ninth Cross-Cultural Research Conference, 2003.

CASE 11

SAMUEL BONNIE: INTERNATIONAL ENTREPRENEUR

ABSTRACT

Emily Devine, an MBA student has just met a successful international entrepreneur and has learned about his company. Emily decides to make this company's decision on a new plant location the subject of her economics paper, giving special consideration to the company's strong focus on social responsibility. Emily must decide which country would be the best choice for the new manufacturing facility, selecting from Indonesia, Cote d'Ivoire, or Moldova.

Introduction

Emily Devine could not stop starring at the customer sitting at table five. She knew it was wrong to stare, but she could not help herself. Ever since the man walked into the café on South Beach, where Emily works to pay for her MBA classes, she could not shake the feeling that she knew this man's face. He was very handsome, perhaps he was a model, or better yet, an actor or musician. It was not unusual to see rich and famous people in the café on Miami Beach. The man was reading some papers that looked very much like a business plan, and Emily nearly dropped the food in his lap as she read over his shoulder while placing his order on the table. All she managed to see was the letterhead SPB International. Again Emily could not help but feel like she knew that name. "Oh well" sighed Emily, "I better forget about him and get back to my work or I will be looking for a new job."

It was not until that night when Emily was researching a paper her economics class that it dawned on her who this man was. "Where did I put that magazine?" she wondered as she searched the piles of books and journals cluttering here desktop. Finally she found it, last month's issue of *Young Entrepreneur*, and there he was on the cover. She recalled reading the article last month and thinking how he was so good-looking, charming and smart. Emily decided that this is whom she would write her report about and sat down to reread the story of SPB International founder, Samuel P. Bonnie.

The Socially Responsible Entrepreneur

Samuel P. Bonnie, Sam to his friends, was just an ordinary guy. He liked to hang out with friends, fish, surf, and when he had a little extra time on his hands, he dappled with molecular chemistry. It was on one of those rainy afternoons in South Florida that Sam made what turned out to be the greatest mistake of his life. It seems that he was fooling around with the properties of foam rubber in order to come up with a better beer coolie to keep his beer cold when he went out fishing. (You know those foam rubber things that people stick beer cans in; they usually have advertising on them.) Sam was trying to develop a liquid that could be put on the foam rubber that would increase its insulation qualities. Sam told the story this way:

> "I was working in my garage lab, and had just put the foam rubber into a tub of the chemical compound when I heard Jack at the door. You all know Jack, Jack Hughes the "American Dream Boy" who won the Gold Medal in cycling at the Olympics in Sydney. I met him when he was in Florida training for the Olympics. Anyway, Jack, who had stopped his training ride because of the rain, and I started talking and watching TV. I think the Wimbledon tournament was on, and I forgot about the experiment in the garage. About an hour later I remembered and ran out to the garage to take the foam rubber out of the solution. The strangest thing had happened. The foam rubber had become hard and what was more peculiar, it had somehow lost over half of its weight. About that time the rain had stopped and Jack decide he was going to head home before it started up again. He was putting his bike helmet on when I got a crazy idea..."

The article recalled how Sam spent the next few weeks fashioning a bicycle helmet out of foam rubber and treating it in the same solution. Jack tried the helmet and liked it so much that he wore it to train, and eventually in the Olympics where he won the Gold. There was a great deal of talk in the cycling world (where events can be won by fractions of a second) about "Mr. Hughes' New Helmet." The article went on to quote Sam on his strong beliefs about social welfare. Emily read this with fascination.

> "It has always bothered me to see companies become rich off the blood and sweat of the third world people. Now do not get me wrong I am not saying that companies should not do business in the third world, I just believe that if they do they should be ethical. Pay the workers a wage that will house and feed a family and do not hire children to work when they should be going to school. I mean this is not rocket science, just treat people with basic respect."

Young Entrepreneur told of how SPB International's plant was one of the first to receive SA 8000 certification for socially responsible manufacturing. SA 8000 certification indicates to the world that the manufacturer who possesses this certification has passed an independent audit of employment practices in areas such as health and safety, discrimination, free association, child labor, working conditions, compensation, and management systems. Employers who are SA 8000 certified agree to pay a living wage, refrain from engaging in forced or child labor, allow employees to join labor unions if they desire, and provide fair and humane working conditions and supervision. The article described how SPB International had recently built a school and a medical clinic at the plant. These facilities were free to workers and their families, as well as other local people.

Jessica Francis and Bryan Saba, the senior partners of Francis & Saba Consulting, had advised SPB International as it was starting out. They both were greatly impressed by Sam's business savvy. "Sam brought us in to advise on several aspects of the business, but in actuality we just confirmed most of his decisions" Saba said when interviewed for the article. "It was amazing," gushed Francis, "I have never seen a new comer to an industry make all the right decisions." Francis and Saba had analyzed the bicycle helmet industry. They had discovered that the global market was $230 million and that there were seven firms in the industry with the top 4 firms claiming $195 million or 85% of the market. Francis and Saba had considered advising Sam not to enter such a concentrated market. "We had prepared our report advising Sam to sell his patent to one of the big boys in the market and to live well on the proceeds until Congress changed everything", Francis remembered.

Jessica Francis was referring to the Bicycle Helmet Act of 2000. In an attempt to lower the staggeringly high number of deaths caused by head trauma resulting from bicycle accidents, and under extreme pressure from the insurance lobby, the United States Congress passed a two-pronged law. The law provided that any state that failed to pass legislation requiring every cyclist to wear a helmet would lose 85% of all federal highway funds it currently received. The bill also allows for tax incentives for companies that produce helmets.

Most of the states were quick to respond, passing laws that fined un-helmeted cyclists from $500 to $5,000. Many of the states offered subsidies to low-income cyclists that would pay up to half the price of a helmet. Sam recalled what happened next.

> "The American market was going to explode, and here I was sitting on a new formula that could produce better lighter helmets at a fraction of the cost. I had to get into the market. But you cannot wade into a market like that a little at a time, you have to jump in, and jump in big. You know like a cannonball. I knew that the current firms in the industry were not going to make it easy for me. But I was the man who designed the helmet that won the Gold Medal and I think maybe I was just too dumb to be scared. I took all of my savings and got a loan from a buddy of mine who had gotten rich during the dot com boom. (He was one of the few who knew when to get out.) I found a place where we could get the helmets produced and then with the help of Jack as a spokesman I started getting these things on the market."

"Boy" Emily thought, "I can't believe this guy. He is so smart and socially minded, yet he is so humble too." Emily read the conclusion of the article, which outlined the success of SPB International. SPB International has already claimed ten percent of the American market and according to Sam they are now looking at new markets.

"We may have gotten lucky with the timing on this thing but

the truth is we have the best product on the market. If it weren't for Congress, we might not have gotten this big this fast, but I think we would have gotten here eventually. We are now moving into the European market. Jack has done a good job as spokesman here in the US for us but in Europe he is very well known, so we are talking to the better known champions of last year's *Tour de France* about endorsement deals. I expect our sales to become huge in Europe. Besides expanding geographically, we are now looking at branching out into the production of motorcycle helmet industry and construction hardhats. And you know, I still need to work on that beer coolie…"

Where to Locate a New Plant

Emily decided that she would use this company as the subject of a paper she needed to write for her economics class. As SPB International expanded, Sam was looking for additional locations in which to establish manufacturing operations. Emily knew from the article that SPB was considering three countries: Indonesia, Cote d'Ivoire (Ivory Coast), and Moldova. An initial investigation into the backgrounds of these countries produced the following information:

INDONESIA

Population	201M (USD)
Population Growth Rate	1.5%
Main Religion	Islam
GDP	142B (USD)
GDP Per Capita	684 (USD)
Life Expectancy	62 years

COTE D'IVOIRE

Population	16.4M (USD)
Population Growth Rate	3.8%
Main Religion(s)	Islam, Christian
GDP	10.4B (USD)
Per Capita GDP	660 (USD)
Life Expectancy	46 years

MOLDOVA

Population	4.28M

Population Growth Rate	.1%
Main Religion	Orthodox
GDP	1.5B (USD)
GDP Per Capita	354 (USD)
Life Expectancy	67 years

As Emily looked over these data it became clear to her that there were perhaps more things to consider in a location decision.

SOURCES

Baye Michael, (2000) <u>Managerial Economics & Business Strategy</u>. Boston, MA:
McGraw-Hill Higher Education.
Pfeffer Jeffrey, (1998) <u>The Human Equation</u>. Boston, MA: Harvard Business School Press.
Social Accountability International's website: http://www.cepaa.org.
State Department Country Background Notes. http://www.state.gov.
Van Horn, James, (2002) <u>Financial Management & Policy</u>. Upper Saddle River, NJ: Prentice Hall.
<u>World Facts and Maps</u>, Rand McNally 2000 Millennium Edition.

This case was prepared by Michael Wilcox, Martine Duchatelet, and Charles Rarick and previously published in the Journal of Knowledge, Culture and Change, 2004.

CASE 12

RED DRAGON ENTERPRISES

ABSTRACT

An Australian manufacturer of industrial batteries enters into a joint venture with a Chinese manufacturer in order to reduce production costs. The Australian firm soon finds that the association is less desirable than had been planned. Chinese government officials appear to be corrupt and local management dishonest. The case explores some of the difficulties that may be found in joint venture operations in China when foreign firms fail to plan, and poorly control their Chinese operations.

Rex Adams is about to leave China and may never return. He has experienced difficulties that he never imaged he would find in a foreign joint venture. His company, Batrionics hoped that China would provide a source of lower cost manufacturing; however, what he found was corrupt government officials, dishonest managers, and poor quality products.

China

The Chinese called their country the "middle kingdom," meaning that China was at the center of the world. For centuries China was in fact the world's leading civilization and sought to keep foreigners out by building a wall thousands of miles long. Although China is officially a communist state, since 1979 the country has been moving towards a capitalistic economy and now eagerly invites foreigners into its economy. The "iron rice bowl," where all workers in China were guaranteed a job, is being replaced by a market-driven system. Although China still has many state-owned enterprises, economic reform is moving rapidly as China becomes a major player in the global marketplace. China became a member of the World Trade Organization in 2001. Having the largest population of any country, with over 1.3 billion, China is often seen as a country with enormous market potential. The cost of labor in many parts of China represents some of the lowest labor costs in the world. China represents the fasting growing economy in the world and many foreign companies have invested in the country in recent years. The large population, and the hope of tapping into that market, as well as those who are looking for a low cost manufacturing location lure many investors. While many investors have found success in China, a number of foreign investors have experienced great difficulties. Batrionics was one those companies which experienced difficulties.

Batrionics

The company was established in 1984 by two Australians as a small manufacturer of laptop computer batteries. Batrionics produced replacement laptop batteries at a cost lower than the original manufacturer and quickly became successful. The batteries were first produced in Australia, and then in Taiwan. When one of the founders died of a sudden heart attack, the remaining founder, Rex Adams, took total control of the business. He expanded the product line into a number of different types of industrial batteries. The industrial battery market is a very competitive one; a market where small price differentials make all the difference. Early in the business the founders learned that if they hoped to be competitive, they would have to move their manufacturing operations out of Australia. Taiwan proved to be a good choice, having much lower production costs and an ability to produce a quality product. The wholly-owned operation in Taiwan was satisfactory for a number of years, however, increased price sensitivities in the market caused Rex to consider other manufacturing locations. An obvious choice was China. Rather than completely shutting down the manufacturing operations in Taiwan and moving them to China, Rex decided to enter into a joint venture agreement with a Chinese manufacturer, and to gradually reduce the company's operations in Taiwan.

Red Dragon Enterprises

After doing some investigation, Rex discovered a small manufacturer of batteries and related industrial products in China called Red Dragon Enterprises. In addition to producing small batteries for the consumer market, Red Dragon also manufactured automotive batteries, watch batteries, switches, timers, electrical cords, smoke alarms, and air purifiers. The company was eager to find a foreign partner who could provide capital for expansion and help the company improve its quality. Red Dragon was considered a quality producer in China, but its products were not of a high enough quality to be sold outside China, with a few exceptions.

The owner of Red Dragon was Tsang Wai. Tsang was a self-made man. After the death of Mao Zedong in 1976, Tsang saw an opportunity in China. With the death of the communist leader he began to manufacturer small electrical products at home, using scrap material from the state-owned factory where he worked. Although this practice was strictly illegal at the time, Tsang did not let that stop him. He moved his manufacturing operations out of his small home when the Chinese government began to allow small businesses to operate legally. At that point he was able to hire workers and expand the product line. Tsang's sales and profits grew rapidly, and being very frugal, he was able to put much money back into the business and grow the company even more. Red Dragon was a respected brand in China but the company had not been successful in exporting its products to the United States and Europe. Some of Red Dragon's products, such as the smoke detectors and water purifiers were sold in some Southeast Asian countries. The company's batteries, however, were not seen as being competitive against international brands.

Rex Adams heard about Red Dragon and was interested in the company because of its experience in producing some of the batteries his company sold. While he was aware of the problems of poor quality, Rex felt that he could install new procedures in the company and improve the company's ability to produce quality batteries. He wanted to find a company that was struggling, and where improvements could be made, because he felt that he could leverage his company's knowledge and skill against the joint venture partner. When Rex approached Tsang, he found a highly motivated and energetic man who was very interested in expanding his operations and becoming a global player. Rex at first referred to Tsang Wai as Mr. Wai, forgetting that in China, the family name comes first and that Tsang Wai would really be Mr. Tsang. The two men got along well, even though Tsang's English proficiency was limited. Tsang had a young assistant who spoke English and who helped him to communicate with Rex. The young assistant would never make eye contact with Rex, and at times, Rex wondered if he was really translating correctly. At one point Rex put his arm around the young man and asked if he was being fair in his translating. His level of discomfort made Rex wonder even more about the translation.

An Agreement is Reached

After a number of trips to China, and many days spent negotiating, the terms of the joint venture were agreed upon. When Rex asked Tsang to sign a contract, he refused. He told Rex that the entire relationship should be based upon trust, and that a contract only represented "paper trust," and would be meaningless. Rex was going to be investing a significant amount of money in the joint venture and felt very uncomfortable doing so without a formal agreement. He told this to Tsang and finally Tsang replied, "OK, we put dragon blood on paper." Not really sure what he meant, Rex felt that this implied that a contact would be created. After still more discussion, and at times argument, the two men agreed to have a simplified document drafted, one which was much more general and open-ended than Rex had planned. He had heard that the Chinese did not like contracts, and that business relationships in China were based on trust and "face" more than legal documents. Although feeling very uneasy about the lack of a detailed formal contract, Rex nevertheless signed what amounted to a general letter of intent. Tsang told Rex that he had recently visited a fortuneteller and that she told him that the joint venture was going to be a "big success." Tsang told Rex that his future in China was bright and that the joint venture would bring both of them good fortune.

At the insistence of Tsang, the joint venture was named Red Dragon Enterprises. Rex had reservations concerning the name, feeling that this would create confusion and not clearly separate the joint venture from Tsang's business. Tsang insisted on the name, telling Rex that the name brought good luck to him and anything else would "encourage evil spirits." The manufacturing operations were located in Nanjing and the agreement would have to be approved by local government officials, or so Rex was told. After Rex had his bank in Australia wire his company's investment to China, Rex and Tsang went to see the government official. Rex was pleased that the government official, Lee Yi, spoke English well. She explained some conditions that would have to be met in order for Batrionics to operate in China. The conditions appeared reasonable to Rex and the meeting went smoothly. Official approval of the joint venture would be made by a committee, Rex was told, and would probably take a few weeks. Rex felt that he was on his way to securing a low cost base of manufacturing.

After two weeks, Rex became concerned when there was no word yet about the government approval of the joint venture. Rex had stayed in China waiting for approval and was getting anxious. Tsang had already begun to spend some of the capital Rex had provided for the partnership, and it was an uncomfortable feeling having the money spent without official approval of the project. Tsang told Rex that there would not be any problems and that the two should continue to plan for expansion. After four weeks of being in China and still no approval, Rex demanded that he and Tsang go to the government official and see what was causing the delay. When they were finally able to get an appointment with Ms. Lee, her disposition did not appear to be as pleasant as before. She told Rex that sometimes these approvals take longer than expected and she felt that the problem with approval was an inadequate level of infrastrure at Red Dragon. When asked for details, Lee told the men that the electrical and water systems of the manufacturing facility were not acceptable, based on government standards. She recommended that Rex hire a contractor to make improvements to these two systems. Rex was concerned that this would delay expansion even further, but Lee told him that she had the name of someone who could do the job quickly and get the plant approved. Rex asked for the name and made the necessary arrangements. Minor improvements were made to the Red Dragon facility, yet the costs appeared not to be minor. Rex agreed to pay the entire costs of the improvements yet he felt that the joint venture was being exploited by the local government.

After another week of waiting, official approval came for the joint venture. Rex was very happy and Tsang commented that although Rex thought it took a long time, it really was expedited because he, Tsang, had "guanxi' or connections. Rex didn't think the process went very quickly and dismissed the guanxi claim. Over the next couple of months Rex made many trips to China and brought managers from Taiwan with him from time to time to consult with the managers at Red Dragon. Additional equipment was purchased, and it finally began to appear that the venture was moving ahead. Tsang informed Rex that the joint venture would need additional capital soon. This came as a complete surprise to Rex as he had planned on not providing any more capital at all for the project. Tsang explained that costs had been higher than expected and that unless additional capital was provided, the quality improvements Rex had demanded could not be achieved. Rex reluctantly agreed to provide more capital

With a business to oversee in Taiwan, Rex left China and spent the next three months between Taiwan and Australia. He left Tsang in charge of the Chinese operation. Tsang made regular reports to Rex, and the reports were always very favorable. Production was increasing, quality was improving, and Red Dragon was about to embark on an international sales drive. Rex began to plan a reduction in the Taiwanese operations as he was going to soon be receiving batteries from China. One of most trusted managers from Taiwan, Chen Wah was asked to visit the Chinese facilities and to measure the progress Red Dragon was making in being able to supply Batrionics with the needed batteries. It was planned that when the facilities in Taiwan were phased out, Chen would still be employed by Batrionics and would help manage the Chinese joint venture.

Bad News from China

Chen traveled to China and made a shocking report to Rex. He had found that the batteries being produced by Red Dragon for Batrionics were not being made of sufficient quality and that production levels were well below what Tsang had reported. Chen also reported that Tsang told him that the joint venture was again almost out of money and would need an additional capital infusion. Rex told Chen to stay in China and to find out all he could about what was happening there. After another week, Chen reported back to Rex that inventory was missing and that he felt some of the managers at Red Dragon had been stealing the product and selling it through Chinese distribution channels. Chen confirmed that the bank account of the joint venture contained almost no funds. Rex decided that he would have to go back to China and see the problems for himself.

When Rex arrived in China, he met with Chen who provided him with the facts that clearly showed that much of the joint venture's inventory was missing. Chen did some checking and found that the products had been sold inside China. It was easy to identify the products made by the joint venture because the products were produced using the new equipment and the equipment left an identifying mark. When Rex presented Tsang with these facts, he said that employees had stolen some of the inventory and that they had all been fired. When asked what happened to the funds in the joint venture bank account, Tsang replied that mistakes had been made in accounting and that he would be investigating what had happened to the money. Rex was very unhappy with the answers provided by Tsang and he lost his temper. He accused Tsang of stealing the money and dealing with him in bad faith. Tsang said nothing and simply looked towards the floor. Rex decided that it was time for legal or governmental action.

Making an appointment with an official at the office of the Commission for Foreign Economic Relations and Trade, Rex hoped to get Chinese governmental help in solving his problems with Tsang. Rex and Chen visited the office of Mr. Wu, who listened to what the two had to say about the situation and he reviewed the joint venture agreement between Batrionics and Red Dragon. He seemed sympathic; however, he offered little advice. After a long period of silence he suggested that Rex hire a consultant, a former official from the Commission to help solve the problems. Rex told Mr. Wu that he was done hiring people recommended by Chinese government officials and that he was going to seek legal assistance in the matter. Both Chen and Mr. Wu recommended against legal action, telling Rex that the joint venture agreement was too weak to be enforced in his favor.

Rex left the government offices wondering how he had ended up in this situation. He knew that other foreign firms were operating in China, and he assumed that they were not experiencing all of these problems, so he wondered why he had such difficulties. Rex had to decide if he should cut his losses and leave China for good, or if he should try to work with Tsang and attempt to salvage the situation.

SOURCES

Ahlstrom, D. M. Young, and A. Nair. (2002). *Deceptive Managerial Practices in China: Strategies for Foreign Firms*. <u>Business Horizons</u>, November-December.
Harris, P. , R. Moran, and S. Moran. (2004). <u>Managing Cultural Differences</u>. Burlington, MA: Elsevier.
Li, J. (2000). <u>Passport China</u>. Novato, CA: World Trade Press.
<u>www.worldfactsandfigures.com/countries/china</u>

This case was prepared by Charles A. Rarick

EXERCISE 7

COMPARATIVE STRATEGY

Purpose: The purpose of this exercise is to develop a better understanding of how organizational strategies differ in Asia, Europe, and the United States.

Procedure: Select one Annual Report from a company headquartered in Asia, Europe, and the United States. In other words, select one Asian, one European, and one American company and find Annual Reports from those companies. Annual Reports can often be downloaded from the company's web site.

Read through the Annual Reports looking for strategic differences that you feel are culturally based. Differences may be found in the importance of market share, profitability, community responsibility, stakeholders, as well as the importance placed on immediate results. Differences in organizational mission and corporate values may also be found.

After doing the analysis, develop a report that highlights your observations.

PART FOUR

INTERNATIONAL STAFFING AND HRM

International staffing issues have become more important with the growth of internationalization and globalization. However, the failure rate of expatriate is still a concern to management. Two important reasons for the failure of expats are personal and family stressors. An additional source of stress originates from cross-cultural differences, such as gender and racial roles, different work ethics, and other variations in culture. The following cases describe the impact of culture on the behavior and attitude of people inside their organizations, as well as the difficulties facing expatriates when they join an organization or attempt to manage and implement organizational changes.

Cases:
A Naïve Sahab in India
Paula Kobe's Sexual Harassment
Hans & Wolfgang Experience American Culture
Ste. Basil Hotel - Moscow
AmeriTech in the Philippines

Exercises:
Which Expatriate to Chose?
Designing a Compensation Package

CASE 13

A NAIVE SAHAB IN INDIA

ABSTRACT

An American manager is selected by his company to improve the operational efficiency of a recently acquired Indian automotive parts company. The manager decides to institute a number of progressive management approaches but finds much resistance from the Indian managers who are expected to implement the changes.

Introduction

It was an opportunity of a lifetime, or so Brian Moseley thought, as he accepted a managing director position for Aspen Automotive's new acquisition in India. Aspen Automotive was a supplier to American automobile manufacturers. The company supplied various component parts for the American automakers, and the recent acquisition of an Indian brake pad company was seen as a keen strategic move for the company. The Bindi Brake Company was an established manufacturer of automotive brake pads which supplied a few European car companies with a high quality product. Competition in this market is fierce and Bindi experienced difficulty in recent years competing with American and Japanese firms. Aspen thought it could capitalize on the experience and low costs of production found in the New Delhi operation and it sent Brian Moseley, an experienced automotive engineer to India to "make the Indians efficient."

Brian and his family quickly adapted to India. Although many expatriates from developed countries experience overwhelming culture shock, the Moseley's assimilated well into the expat community of New Delhi. With the help of personal assistants and children in private schools, the Moseley's could separate themselves from most of the challenges of everyday life in urban India. Although they sometimes missed some of the things they took for granted back in the United States, they enjoyed the standard of living they were experiencing as privileged expatriates in India. Brian knew that his job responsibilities were to turn around the newly acquired Indian operation, and that if he did this within two years, he would be promoted and moved back to U.S. He felt that this assignment could greatly advance his career.

Managers at Aspen's corporate headquarters felt that the introduction of certain Western managerial practices would be beneficial to Bindi and improve overall efficiency and profitability. Brian was selected to direct the organizational change effort due to his past record of accomplishments in the U.S. and abroad. He had been successful in the turnaround of troubled parts manufacturing plants in Louisville, Kentucky and Toledo, Ohio. Additionally, he worked internationally in Canada, Mexico, and Brazil. Aspen felt that his MBA in management from Michigan State, coupled with his previous domestic and international experience made him a suitable person to direct the Indian change management strategy.

Need for Change

Although Bindi produced reasonably high quality brake components, and labor costs were exceptionally low, the overall efficiency of the operation was considerably below other Aspen plants. Top management felt that if the Indian operation could match the level of efficiency of even the least efficient American plant, the acquisition would be a success. After an initial plant visit, top management concluded that the plant was crippled with bureaucracy and that there was no incentive for exceptional performance. Aspen managers observed what they felt were too many Bindi employees drinking tea and socializing instead of working at a regular pace. They were also shocked to find that no Bindi employee ever received a performance review and that pay for performance was never even considered by past management. Bindi employees were seldom discharged, even when they were clearly not well suited to their jobs and performed poorly. Pay increases and other rewards were administered on the basis of seniority. Employees were often selected, not based on their abilities or potential, but because they were related to a current employee of Bindi. The number of sick days and personal days requested were well above the average of the other Aspen plants.

Brian was directed to make the India subsidiary more like the rest of the Aspen corporate family. For the first three months Brian did little more than observe and learn about the current managerial practices of Bindi. He spoke with managers, and employees alike, and made mental notes of the experiences. Brian identified employees whom he felt should be replaced and also identified employees whom he felt had the greatest potential for advancement. After this initial three-month investigation, Brian met with his senior managers at Bindi and proposed that they collectively formulate a turnaround strategy. All of Bindi's managers were Indians and most had been educated in Indian universities. One manager, Rajan Patel had studied in London and received a postgraduate diploma from the University of London in economics. Brian felt that Rajan was one of the most promising candidates for advancement and he hoped that Rajan would take the lead in structuring the change management program.

Brian's Frustration

Although Brian had hoped that the Indian managers would formulate a plan for change among themselves, he increasingly became frustrated after a month when no one came forth to recommend a plan. Brian suggested to the group that they should consider changes such as pay for performance programs, annual performance reviews, management by objectives, and perhaps a 360-degree performance appraisal program. He felt that if the group emphasized performance appraisal that many of Bindi's efficiencies would disappear. Brian felt that most of the employees had the potential for great improvement and that all they needed was a better system of management. A more scientific and objective approach to management, coupled with a more participative approach would succeed in increasing the efficiencies and ultimate success of Bindi.

Over the next several months Brian became increasingly dissatisfied with the progress of the India managers in achieving any constructive plan for changing Bindi's managerial practices. His frustration level at times became high and he openly expressed his disapproval through anger. At times Brian would criticize members of his managerial team in front of their subordinates. The relationship between Brian and the managers became increasingly strained and he was being referred to behind his back as "sahab" or "big boss". A throwback to the British colonial days, this term was used in some instances to refer to a manager who had little understanding of Indian culture.

One of Brian's biggest critics was Rajan Patel. Rajan often criticized Brian's managerial style as being too direct and forceful. On at least occasion Rajan referred to Brian's tactics as "culturally imperialistic" and he felt that Brian was too immature to be the managing director. He was concerned that Brian was trying to change India's culture to fit an American model of management. Although educated in the West, Rajan did not feel that Indian employees were receptive to many managerial practices which ran counter to basic cultural values. He openly questioned Brian and Aspen's approaches to changing the culture of the Bindi Brake Company.

Brian Takes Charge

After seven months in India Brian decided that if change were to occur, he would have to be the one to initiate the change. He called his senior managers into his office one morning and told them of the following changes which were to be made effective immediately. First, Brian announced that Prakash Nur, the assistant plant director and most senior manager would be replaced by C.P. Rao. Rao was a young engineer educated at an American university and a person who Brian felt would be best able to implement his vision of change at Bindi. Second, Brian announced that performance appraisals would begin immediately and that at least two employees in each work group should be eliminated in the interest of organizational efficiency. Third, a new plan of 360 degree feedback would be implemented and that subordinates would evaluate their superiors, and that annual compensation increases would be contingent of these reviews. No annual increases in compensation would be automatic, and all raises would now be based on merit. Finally, all personal assistants (chaprasi) would be fired and their responsibilities assumed by the managers themselves. Even though the salary expense of the personal assistants was small, Brian felt that it created an unnecessary administrative level and no other Aspen unit allowed such positions.

The Indian managers at first seemed stunned by Brian's mandates. No one spoke and a dead silence seemed to fill the room. When Brian asked for feedback on his "recommendations" the managers looked down at the table in front of them and said nothing. Prakash who got up and left the room broke the silence. Later, a few of the managers politely told Brian that the ideas were too bold and too sudden a change for Bindi. Brian angrily responded that the change was long overdue and that anyone who would not go along with the new plan should leave the company.

Much grumbling was taking place over the next few days at Bindi as the managers announced the changes. Brian learned that Prakash had resigned and that Rajan was telling everyone of his dissatisfaction with

Brian's managerial style. Brian decided to talk individually with all the managers and started with Rajan. The meeting was less than cordial and ended with Brian's warning Rajan that he "better come on board soon" or that he too would be replaced. During the subsequent meetings with all the Indian managers, Brian tried to convince them of the urgency and necessity of these proposed changes. At times it seemed as if they agreed with him and he felt that finally change would occur. After all, when directly asked, no one told him that they would not implement the changes.

After a week and no changes were taking place, Brian reasoned it might take a little longer than he thought due to cultural constraints. He was, however, critical of Rajan who he felt might sabotage the change effort. Brian keep a close eye on Rajan and one morning he was told that Rajan would not be in the office for a week because his brother was getting married in Bombay. Brian was suspicious and checked the personnel records and discovered that Rajan did not have any brothers. He waited for Rajan to return and then asked him where he had been. Rajan replied that he had attended the wedding of his brother in Bombay. Brian, outraged by the lie immediately fired him on the spot. Rajan left without a word spoken to Brian.

Now What?

Although things seemed to be a bit tense at Bindi, Brian told himself that change is difficult and that the long run consequences would be good for Aspen, Bindi, and India. He continued to quiz the managers on their progress towards the change efforts and was told that all changes were being implemented as he had instructed. Further investigation revealed that no changes were being made. Brian called for another meeting of his managers and was shocked to learn that a number of them had decided to quit rather than attend the meeting. Included in the group which resigned was C.P. Rao, whom Brian was convinced would be a leader in his vision of change at Bindi. Brian sat alone in his office wondering if change would ever come to the Bindi Brake Company.

This case was prepared by Charles A. Rarick and previously published in the International Journal of Case Studies.

CASE 14

PAULA KOBE'S HARASSMENT IN BRAZIL

ABSTRACT

A recent MBA graduate lands her dream job in Sao Paulo working as a consultant in the Brazilian office of an American company. While she finds the job and country to be very interesting, unexpected challenges, mainly sexual harassment, make the assignment too difficult to handle. The case explores cross-cultural gender roles and legal issues in international assignments.

The thought of being assigned to Brazil fresh out of her MBA program was a dream come true for Paula Kobe. Paula had been offered a job with Behavioral Management Systems (BMS) upon graduation from Duke University, where she graduated with an MBA in management. It was her dream to work abroad, and she was especially excited about the offer made by BMS to work in Brazil as a consultant. Paula had studied for a year in Portugal as an undergraduate student and was almost fluent in Portuguese. The assignment in Sao Paulo seemed to an ideal situation. Unfortunately, the assignment presented challenges she had not expected.

Paula Kobe worked four years after earning her undergraduate degree in engineering before attending graduate school. With the failure of her marriage, Paula felt that it was a good time to change her life, and she was seeking something new and exciting. Behavioral Management Systems was headquartered in Atlanta and had offices in Mexico, Venezuela, Chile, and Brazil. The company specialized in providing management and teamwork consulting, and also provided some consulting services in quality management. Paula would be providing Brazilian firms advice on achieving ISO 9000 certification and in improving the quality of their manufacturing processes. Her engineering background, coupled with her management training, made for a good fit in this area of consulting.

A New Life in Sao Paulo

BMS had offered Paula an attractive compensation package, one that would allow her to live quite well as an expatriate in Brazil. She was able to rent a large, luxury apartment in an upscale part of town and hire a maid/cook, something she had never thought she could afford. While the job responsibilities were of interest to her, and the compensation was appealing, Paula did realize that she would be giving up contact with her friends and boyfriend back in the United States. Adjusting to the culture of Brazil was not especially difficult for Paula. She had traveled abroad quite a bit, including vacationing in Rio de Janeiro, and she was somewhat familiar with Brazilian culture. BMS had allowed Paula two weeks to become familiar with Sao Paulo and the company before giving her any significant responsibility. During her first two weeks Paula learned about company policy, Brazilian business, and made many calls back to the United States. She had planned for her boyfriend to visit her in Brazil every month, and she would fly back to the U.S. every month, reducing the time apart to only two weeks. With a maid and someone to cook her food, international television, and an interesting job, Paula felt good about being in Brazil.

Rafael Scarado

After two weeks of orientation and getting to know the company, Paula was ready to be assigned to her work area. She would be working in the Quality Improvement Division and she would be reporting to Rafael Scarado. Rafael was the head of the smallest of BMS's divisions and was responsible for Paula's training. Although Paula had studied quality management at Duke, BMS had a proprietary system that all new employees had to learn and implement.

When Paula first met Rafael she concluded that, while he was a very pleasant man, his orientation towards women was typical of most Brazilian men. Paula thought that Rafael was too forward towards her and that she would have to gradually train him in how to treat women. For example, when they first met, Rafael immediately asked Paula how old she was and when Paula responded that she was 29, Rafael patted her on the cheek and said "such a baby." Rafael's English was very good since he had studied for four years in the United States and worked in Canada. Rafael grew up poor in the old capital of Brazil, Salvador, and was fortunate enough to earn a soccer scholarship to a small midwestern college in Illinois. A chance encounter with a soccer coach from a small college in Illinois was only the beginning of Rafael's luck. After college, Rafael was offered a position by a trustee of the college to work for an affiliate of the trustee's company in Canada. Rafael had studied mathematics and business administration in college, and the trustee felt that this background would be helpful in creating a new quality management program at the Canadian facility. Rafael had been a star soccer player in college and was quite good with interpersonal relations. The trustee liked Rafael and had confidence in his abilities. Rafael worked in Canada for three years before returning to Brazil. In Canada, Rafael met his wife and now lives with her in Sao Paulo with their three children.

Uncomfortable Encounters

One of the first things that Paula told her friends back in the U.S. about her job was the fact that her boss, Rafael would greet her in the morning with a kiss on the cheek. Paula knew that this was not uncommon in Brazil, nevertheless, it made her uncomfortable. She wanted to tell Rafael that she did not want him to greet her this way but she worried that he might be offended and so decided to put up with it for the time being. Rafael provided good conversation for Paula and her friends when Paula called them to recount her experiences in Brazil. Her friends began calling Rafael her "Latin lover." It appeared to Paula that Rafael had a romantic interest in her because he would spend much time asking her about her personal life and staring into her eyes. These long stares also made Paula uncomfortable. It appeared to Paula that Rafael was a caring person and an understanding trainer, but she worried that his attention and concern may be more related to his romantic interest in her. She felt that if she offended Rafael that he might not be as helpful in her career development.

As time progressed the level of discomfort began to increase. In addition to the good morning kiss, Rafael would touch Paula from time to time when making a point. He would put his hands on her shoulders, touch her arm, brush her hair, and hold her hand. Paula became increasingly troubled by Rafael's actions and decided that she should find a way of letting him know that this behavior was not welcomed. At one point Paula asked Rafael if his wife knew about your flirting at the office. Rafael just laughed and responded, "She knows how romantic Brazilian men can be." Mentioning his wife did not seem to have much effect on Rafael's behavior, so Paula thought she might have to come up with another approach. She wasn't sure what that would be, but she put it aside as she planned for the upcoming visit of her boyfriend.

A Visitor from America

Although Paula had planned on returning to the United States every two weeks, this plan proved impractical. The time required for travel and her busy training schedule were not compatible. It was decided that Paula's boyfriend, Shane, would visit her. Rafael had agreed to give Paula an extended weekend so the "two lovers could make up for lost time." Paula appreciated the understanding of Rafael, and she also hoped that he would get the message that she was involved with someone else and not interested in his advances.

Shane arrived in Sao Paulo and Paula could not wait to see him and tell him about her new life in Brazil. She wanted to show him around the country but the limited amount of time Shane could stay prohibited that from happening. The two explored Sao Paulo and discussed their future together. Throughout the visit Paula did not give a thought to Rafael and the problems she was having with him. On the last night of Shane's visit Paula finally mentioned, "The guy who is training me seems to be in love with me." This statement caught Shane's attention and he pressed for more details. Paula explained what Rafael would do that made her uncomfortable and Shane insisted that she tell him to stop, or that she tell Rafael's superior about "the sexual harassment." Paula told Shane not to worry and that it was "no big deal." She told him that Brazil was different from the United States and that she could handle it. Although Shane was worried, he had confidence in Paula's judgment and the issue was not discussed further.

Short Skirts Make for Good Business

Paula returned to BMS refreshed from her short vacation and ready to complete her training. She was looking forward to actually working with clients and getting out into the field. When she saw Rafael on her first day back, he kissed her on the cheek and asked her how she enjoyed the weekend. She responded that it was wonderful and she mentioned Shane by name many times. Rafael told her that he was surprised that she looked so rested. When asked why, Rafael told her "surely the two lovers spent the entire nights making love." Paula was embarrassed and not sure what to say so, she decided to change the conversation to a work matter.

After another week, Paula was ready for her first assignment. She and

Rafael would be visiting the offices of a medium-sized manufacturer in hopes of landing a quality improvement contract. Paula was excited about the upcoming visit and prepared her part of the presentation with great diligence. Rafael coached her on some parts of the presentation and she felt confident that she was ready to make what amounted to a sales call on the client.

During the presentation Rafael played a dominant role. It appeared that he wanted to make it clear that he was in charge of the presentation. Since it was Paula's first presentation for BMS, she allowed Rafael to do most of the talking, and to interrupt her during her presentation. The client seemed very interested in what BMS could do for his company in terms of team building and continuous improvement efforts. Paula felt as if the presentation was a success. No contract was signed that day, however, Paula felt that BMS had made a good impression and that surely they would get the contract.

On the way back to the office, Rafael told Paula that she did a good job and that he would be relaying that information back to management. He praised her presentation skills and complimented her preparation. Rafael told Paula that he was confident that if she had just worn a shorter skirt they would have signed a contract immediately with the prospective client. Paula laughed, assuming that this was just another one of Rafael's attempt at humor, but Rafael was not laughing. When she asked him if he was serious, he replied that he was very serious. Rafael told Paula that he watched the client look at her, and that since she was "a very beautiful woman," she should use this to her advantage. In Rafael's words "short skirts make for good business in Brazil." Paula could not believe what she was hearing. She felt that Rafael was trying to exploit her, and that he really didn't care that she had an MBA and a skill set that was useful to her job.

The drive back to the office was an uncomfortable one with Paula remaining silent most of the time. Later that evening, when Paula called her friends back in the U.S., she told them about the incident and that she felt that Rafael was only interested in "pimping her out." Her friends suggested that she bring a charge of sexual harassment against Rafael and the company. Paula wasn't sure what to do. She wondered what would happen to her career if she protested Rafael's action, and she wondered if what he was doing was illegal. Paula thought about her job, her apartment and maid, and her head was spinning. She went to sleep that night anxious and pondering her next move.

This case was prepared by Charles A. Rarick

CASE 15

HANS AND WOLFGANG EXPERIENCE AMERICAN CULTURE

ABSTRACT

Two German expatriates are assigned to a newly formed strategic alliance with a company in the United States. They experience difficulty with American culture and the culture of the organization. Although they achieve some success in their assignment, the two men leave the company a year early and return to Germany. The case explores possible areas of conflict between German and American culture.

In an effort to gain a competitive advantage in the increasingly competitive information technology (IT) marketplace, Business Software Solutions, Inc (BSS) of Lexington, Kentucky and ABBA Deutschland of Stuttgart, Germany decided to form a strategic alliance. Both firms felt as if they could gain from the partnership by combining the narrow expertise and competitive advantage they had developed in their fields. Business Software Solutions was founded by Jim Gibson, a former professor of engineering at the University of Kentucky who developed a number of business applications software packages in an era when few existed. The company grew rapidly, and was very profitable from its inception. From basic software development, BSS has expanded more into serving the IT needs of medium and large-sized companies. ABBA Deutschland is a large German multinational company with a specialization in satellites and data transmission. ABBA is considered one of Europe's leading information and communications companies, yet it lacks the software development capabilities it needs and must subcontract much of this important function. It was felt that the creation of a partnership between BSS and ABBA would be beneficial to both firms, but that the partnership should begin slowly.

The Germans Arrive

It was decided that two technical managers from Germany would be assigned to the Kentucky company for a period of two years. Hans Reinhardt and Wolfgang Reinhardt (not related) were chosen to work at BSS in Lexington to help develop the strategic alliance. It was hoped that the two-man team could learn about BSS's software development process and act as a liaison between the two firms. Both Hans and Wolfgang were software engineers who graduated from the same prestigious technical university in Germany with a degree in software engineering. They both also attended Stuttgart Institute of Management and Technology and earned advanced degrees in information systems and management. As part of their academic studies, the pair completed an extensive internship at Cisco Systems GmbH. Both men were single and looked forward to living in the United States for the two year assignment. The boyhood friends loved to travel and hoped to see more of the United States during their short stay in the United States.

BSS provided Hans and Wolfgang with a furnished apartment. Because the two of them wanted to live together, BSS felt that they could provide more upscale living facilities. The apartment was in a luxurious complex 20 minutes from BBS headquarters. The two men also decided to lease one automobile, and they decided on a 7 series BMW. It seemed like the two-year stay would be very enjoyable for the two of them.

Hans and Wolfgang immediately began to impress the people at BSS. They were quite motivated and appeared to be technically very competent. After only one week at BBS, Hans was able to suggest an improvement in a software design that would save BBS a considerable amount of money. The two men appeared eager to make a large contribution to the strategic alliance. While their part was mostly technical, they were also to report back to Germany on the progress of the partnership.

Most of the employees at BSS found the Germans interesting. While the city of Lexington was diverse (at least for Kentucky) due to the fact that the University of Kentucky was located there and attracted more foreign-born residents, not many Germans lived there. While the employees of BSS were interested in the two men, not everyone found them likable. Many employees reported to Sam Sherwin, Hans and Wolfgang's supervisor and a member of middle management, that the men were "kinda stuffy" and that they "keep to themselves too much." Some of their co-workers resented the fact that the two men keep the doors to their offices closed while they were inside working. It appeared that they did not want to interact much with others.

While everyone at BSS was on a first name basis, Hans and Wolfgang always introduced themselves as "Reinhardt." Since they both had the same last name, this created some confusion. The two were given nicknames by one of the employees and those nicknames caught on quickly. Hans was called "Hands" and Wolfgang was called "Wolfie." While the two Germans responded to the nicknames, it sometimes appeared that they did not appreciate their new American names. Most BSS employees found Hans and Wolfgang to be pleasant, but they were not quite as friendly as most of the employees, who, were mostly from central Kentucky.

Hans and Wolfgang were assigned to work on a project with three American engineers. The project was directly related to the work BSS had been doing for ABBA on a contract basis. The software application for an advanced personal data transmission system had presented the engineers at BSS with many difficulties. With the help of the German engineers, especially Hans, the team was able to overcome the most significant difficulties and move the project mostly towards closure.

Assigned to Colin

Sam decided that Hans' early success should be leveraged into a new project being directed by Colin Corum. Colin had just graduated from the University of Kentucky with a degree in computer science and he was very young, however, Sam believed that Colin showed great promise. He had made a significant amount of money while still a college student working as an independent contractor for some of the biggest names in software design. Although it was rumored that Colin had made over a million dollars while a college student, the fact that he was working at BSS made others think that he may not be wealthy. Colin was offered jobs at more prestigious companies, however he wanted to remain in Lexington and this limited his opportunities.

When Sam approached Hans with the idea that he work with Colin on another, bigger project, Hans suggested that he and Wolfgang both be assigned to the project. Although Sam felt that Wolfgang could be better used elsewhere, he agreed, reasoning that the two men were insecure living and working in a new country. Hans and Wolfgang did not have much respect for Colin. They had interacted with him briefly on the earlier assignment and felt that he was not capable of leading a team of engineers. Although only a few years separated Colin from the Germans, Hans and

Wolfgang felt that Colin was very immature. They would be reporting to him and he would be reporting on their progress to Sam. Although the men felt uncomfortable with this assignment, they nevertheless agreed to Sam's suggestion.

Colin was a very talented software engineer, but some of his personal habits were a bit unconventional. For example, he frequently brought his dog to the office with him, an office that looked more like a sports memorabilia store, featuring his favorite team – the University of Kentucky basketball team. The office was very cluttered and his personal appearance was less than professional, at least from the eyes of Hans and Wolfgang. The two German's felt that Colin was too young and immature to be in such a responsible position. They had great respect for Sam, so they tolerated the quirks of Colin and tried to work with him.

Colin referred to the two men by their newly acquired nicknames, as did most BSS employees. He seemed to have some respect for Hans, but paid little attention to Wolfgang. As the days and weeks went by, Wolfgang began to miss work sporadically, complaining about allergies and bad headaches. Colin didn't seem to mind that Wolfie wasn't around and assigned more work to Hans. Hans didn't seem to mind the additional workload and defended Wolfgang whenever Colin made negative comments about Wolfgang.

Cultural Differences

Sam would on occasion stop by to see how the expatriates were doing, and perhaps sensed that things weren't going too well. He invited Hans, Wolfgang, and Colin to join him at an Irish pub near work for dinner and a night of drinking. The evening went well, at first. Sam asked Hans and Wolfgang to talk about Germany and how their country was different from the United States. Hans and Wolfgang also talked about how ABBA was different from BSS. At first the Germans appeared to be somewhat tense, especially Wolfgang, but as time went on all four men became relaxed and joked about many things. As Wolfgang drank more beer he became bolder and began to provide a "German perspective on America." He told some jokes about Americans and explained how Germans respected Americans, but felt that they were not very cultured, were undisciplined, and did not take a world-view, and instead thought everything resolved around the United States. Wolfgang also complained about the lack of respect many Americans had for society. He explained for example that "someone with a punk automobile and very loud music invades the personal space of others." It appeared that Colin did not appreciate the cross-cultural analysis provided by Wolfgang and made some derogatory comments about Nazi's and World War II. Although there was some tension at times, the beer flowed freely; the men laughed, and it appeared, left the pub on good terms.

After about six months at BSS, Hans asked Sam if the two men could take a few days off. He told Sam that he and Wolfgang had some friends in Florida and they wanted to visit them. Sam told Hans that he would have to check with Colin since he was the project manager. When asked, Colin refused to grant the time off. Colin told Hans that he was about to assign him a very important part of the project they were working on and that it was important that the team show early progress. He told Hans that "if Wolfie picked up some of the slack" the team would be making more progress. Besides, he said, BSS was receiving a number of orders for software development from ABBA that they had not anticipated, and the firm would need both of them to work extra hours to help with the new business. Hans mildly protested, but Colin would not budge on his decision. After a discussion with Wolfgang, the two men decided to approach Sam about the time off request. Sam reaffirmed the need for everyone to work more hours but agreed to talk with Colin. After a short time, Sam told Hans and Wolfgang that they could take a Friday off and have a three-day weekend. The Germans thanked Sam and began planning their trip. They drove the next weekend to Florida, picking up two speeding tickets, and arrived at work the following Monday exhausted, and less than friendly.

Problems Continue

Tensions between Colin and Wolfgang continued, and it was clear to everyone at BSS that the two did not like each other very much. Sam felt that Wolfgang was a hard worker, but that he was not as talented an engineer as Hans. His personality was more stoic, and he was very formal and didn't smile very much. Sam had told Colin to work with Wolfgang in improving their relationship because the partnership was very important to BSS, and Hans was needed in the coming months to handle projects which no one at BSS was capable of doing.

With increased business coming in, it was clear that BSS would need more software engineers. Sam decided that it might be a good time to have a meeting with Colin, Hans, and Wolfgang to discuss how things were going, and to see about the possibility of bringing more ABBA engineers to BSS. Sam had already decided to hire more American engineers, but he also wanted to get ABBA engineers involved in the projects. The meeting was scheduled for 1 P.M. and Hans and Wolfgang arrived promptly. Sam entered the meeting room a few minutes later and the three men began talking. Hans told Sam that in Germany it is customary for employees to take an entire month off from work during the summer months. Sam chuckled and said that maybe he should be assigned to ABBA for a while. By 1:15 P.M. Wolfgang was beginning to appear upset. He kept looking at his watch and said nothing. A few minutes later he told Sam that he didn't know if he could work any longer with Colin. When Sam asked why, Wolfgang proceeded to list the many concerns he had about the young manager. Wolfgang told Sam that Colin was immature, that he didn't respect the education and training of Hans and himself, and that Colin was intentionally giving him work that was not challenging and that he knew Wolfgang would dislike. Hans said nothing but appear not to disagree with what Wolfgang was saying. At that moment, Colin arrived for the meeting. He apologized for being late, and explained that he was on the telephone with an important customer.

Sam thought that it might be a good idea not to discuss the tension between Wolfgang and Colin at this time and proceeded to talk about the upcoming workload. He explained to the three men how work orders were increasing, and that BSS would need o hire more engineers. Sam asked if ABBA would be willing to send additional engineers to Lexington. Both German men felt that it would be possible, and also a good idea to bring in more Germans. Hans volunteered to contact ABBA and make an informal inquiry about this possibility. The meeting ended without any further discussion of the tensions between Colin and Wolfgang.

Things continued as usual at BSS. The workload increased and tensions were sometimes high between Wolfgang and Colin. The Germans tried to enjoy their time in Kentucky by taking road trips on the weekends and making new American friends. Two additional engineers would be coming from ABBA and Sam felt that this addition might help reduce some of the difficulties between Colin and Wolfgang. Sam also increased the pay of all members of the special project team headed by Colin due to their increased workload. He felt that this might also help in easing the strain experienced by all.

Goodbye to America

Upon the approach of their one-year anniversary at BSS, Hans and

Wolfgang requested a meeting with Sam. He assumed that the men wanted to talk about the upcoming arrival of the two additional German expatriates. The meeting instead was about Hans and Wolfgang returning to Germany. Hans explained that he and Wolfgang were returning to Germany, but that they would stay two weeks after the new expatriates arrived to help them settle in and get use to their new surroundings. Sam was shocked and very disappointed. He had actually hoped that Hans, especially, would decide to stay even longer than the planned two years. The two men thanked Sam for allowing them to work for BSS and they told him that they had enjoyed their experiences in America, however, they were anxious to return to Germany. Sam asked if there was anything he could do to change their minds, but the Germans appeared not to be flexible on the issue. Sam shook their hands and said that he hoped that he would be able to visit them in Germany. As the men left his office, Sam sat, wondering how he was going to replace Hans, and if he should have managed the German engineers differently.

SOURCES

Crane, R. (2000). European Business Cultures. Essex: Pearson Educational, Limited.

Flamini, R. (1997). Passport Germany. San Rafael, CA: World Trade Press.

Scarborough, J. (2001). The Origins of Cultural Differences and Their Impact on Management. Westport, CT: Quorum Books.

This case was prepared by Charles A. Rarick.

CASE 16

STE. BASIL HOTEL-MOSCOW

Struggling with Cultural Values in a Post-Communist State

ABSTRACT

This case profiles the difficulties experienced by an American expatriate operating a luxury hotel in Russia. The American general manager is confronted with problems of employee motivation, poor customer service, corruption, and the possible loss of the hotel to its Russian partner.

It was a typical October day in Moscow as Greg Hill looked out the window of his office in the Ste. Basil Hotel. As he saw the snow begin to fall he realized that it was going to be a very long, cold winter in Russia and he longed for the sunshine and warmth of his previous assignment in Miami Beach. While the move to Moscow had been a difficult experience, he and his wife had adjusted reasonably well, and Greg felt that the move would position him for advancement in his American company. He felt that the hardship of living in Russia would be offset by advancement opportunity, however, he was now very concerned with about his future. A deeply religious man, Greg began to pray for a solution to his problems.

The Ste. Basil Hotel

The Ste. Basil Hotel of Moscow is a 4-star hotel located in Red Square. The idea for a luxury hotel was conceived by Louis Cunningham, who was the CEO of LCC Properties. LCC owned a number of luxurious hotel properties in the United States, Canada, South America, and Japan. Cunningham developed the idea for a luxury hotel after a visit to Russia in 1994 in which he and his wife toured the former communist state. Cunningham noticed that the quality of hotels in the country was poor, most being old Soviet style in appearance and operations. Cunningham knew that a number of American and European businesspeople were traveling to Russia, and that an opportunity existed for a hotel that matched the level of quality found in the West. On subsequent visits Cunningham spotted an abandoned construction site near St. Basil Cathedral and decided that it would be a prime location for a luxury hotel. The site was owned by the Russian government who agreed to provide the site if LCC would invest the necessary $50 million to develop it into a 4-star property. The Russian government also insisted that LCC create a partnership with the state-owned airline that would take 51% ownership of the operation. Although Cunningham didn't like the idea of minority interest in the project, he was excited about the location, and even more excited about the prospect of being a pioneering capitalist in a former Communist country.

With the fall of the Soviet Union in 1991, Western business began to take in interest in the former Communist state. The reform movement begun by Mikhail Gorbachev would eventually result in the collapse of the Soviet Union, and the satellite states would gain their independence. The early reform movement of glasnost or "openness" resulted in the lifting of censorship, the release of dissidents, and greater tolerance for religious freedom. Glasnost was followed by perestroika or "restructuring" in which the economy was decentralized and privatized. Military spending was cut and free elections were held. As the former Communist superpower turned towards capitalism Western businesses looked for opportunities.

A Luxury Hotel in Moscow

Louis Cunningham was one of those seeking this new opportunity. Although Cunningham was extremely excited about the project and had a particular interest in seeing a capitalistic spirit come to Russia, he was forced to delegate most responsibilities for the new venture due to the failing health of his wife. The new hotel was named the Ste. Basil due to its proximity to St. Basil Cathedral. Cunningham chose the abbreviation "Ste." because he thought it would "add class" and provide the luxury image the hotel sought to project. Cunningham selected Greg Hill to be the general manager of the new hotel and to oversee completion of the construction of the facility. Greg Hill was a 47-year-old general manager of a luxury hotel in Miami Beach, Florida. He had worked for LCC since graduating from a small college in the Midwest with a degree in hospitality administration. Hill and his wife who were raised in St. Louis, Missouri had moved a number of times as Greg gained increasingly responsible positions with LCC. With their two children away at college, the Hill's felt that moving abroad would be less difficult than it had been when the children were younger. They did enjoy living in Miami and hoped to retire to south Florida at a later date. The opportunity to build and manage a new hotel in a former communist country was an offer that Greg felt he could not turn down. He felt that success in this project could move him into the ranks of upper management at LCC. Mrs. Hill was a teacher in Miami and enjoyed other cultures. She looked forward to living in a foreign country, and in fact often felt that moving to Miami was like living in a different country. The Hill's were friendly people, and although not considered worldly, they were open to new experiences and adjusted to new situations well.

The move to Moscow and the completion of the hotel's construction provided many unforeseen difficulties, but the Russian partners were helpful in overcoming most obstacles. Greg Hill developed the Ste. Basil into a fine hotel. The hotel stood out in great contrast to the poorly equipped and managed hotels which were remnants of the Soviet era. The Ste. Basil provided its guests with an outstanding restaurant and café, an indoor pool, an exercise facility, a dry cleaning service, satellite television, modem/data portals, conference rooms, currency exchange, a gift shop, and concierge services. The rooms were clean, modern, and spacious. The hotel catered to foreign businesspeople from the United States and Europe and was one of the highest priced hotels in Moscow. Rack room rates ranged from $215-450US per night. Conference facilities could also be rented and the hotel provided a catering service to conference participants. With increasing business between Russia and the West it was felt that the Ste. Basil would be the obvious choice among business travelers.

Recruitment of Employees

The Ste. Basil would have to fill all positions, with the exception of general manager, with local labor. Since Greg Hill was the only American expatriate, he felt that he should be actively involved in the recruitment and selection process. With the help of his Russian partners, Hill placed an advertisement in the Moscow Times for all hotel positions. The advertisement was in English since it had been decided that all employees should be proficient in the English language. Response to the advertisement was overwhelming. Thousands of people arrived to apply for the positions. Many of the people who sought employment at the Ste. Basil were educated beyond job requirements. The Ste. Basil received applications from scientists, attorneys, doctors, professors, writers, as well as recent university graduates. Greg was told that the applicants could make much more money working for an American company than continuing in their present professions.

Greg was assisted in applicant screening by his assistant general manager. Victor Popov was appointed by the Russian partners to act not only as the assistant general manager, but also to help Greg with his assimilation and understanding of Russian culture. Victor had a one time been employed in the airline industry as an engineer. He held degrees in engineering, including a master's degree in radio engineering from the St. Petersburg Electrotechnical University. Victor's great grandfather had been a pioneer in the development of radio and the family name was well respected in Russia. Victor spoke fluent English and German, in addition to his native Russian. His hotel experience was limited to a short assignment in an East German hotel, and it was never clear to Greg what his responsibilities were in that assignment. Greg and Victor went through each application and began eliminating individuals who were clearly not qualified. Anyone who had previous hotel experience was eliminated from further consideration. It was felt that these employees had acquired bad habits working for state-owned hotels and it would be very difficult to retrain them. The only exceptions would be for critical positions such as chef which required previous experience. Victor strongly suggested that older applicants (over 35 years of age) should also not be selected. Greg was not sure about this request, but he deferred to Victor's judgment. Greg, however, refused to follow Victor's advice and eliminate all female applicants with small children. Greg did eliminated anyone who had an advanced degree such as an attorney, scientist, or physician, feeling that such a person would become quickly dissatisfied with the position.

After the initial screening applicants were invited for an interview. This proved difficult since many of the applicants did not have a telephone and could not be reached except by mail. Greg decided to eliminate those candidates since the applicant pool was more than sufficient. When word got out that the hotel was interviewing, some of the applicants without telephones walked in and requested interviews. Victor granted some of these applicants interview appointments. The interviewing and selection process took two weeks and included structured and unstructured questions, questions asking applicants to provide their recommendations to hypothetical problems they might experience on the job, a written test of English ability, and a short intelligence test (in English). For the most part Greg was discouraged by the responses of the applicants, especially the responses to the unstructured and situational questions. Many of the applicants proved very short answers or were unable to answer at all. These applicants were eliminated from further consideration. In the end, however, Greg and Victor were able to assemble a workforce which both felt would be satisfactory.

Orientation and Training

A mandatory three-day orientation session was conducted for all employees. The orientation program provided employees with information on LCC Enterprises such as its history and mission, basic training on the importance of customer service, grooming, manners, and company policy. After the three-day orientation program, specific job training was provided. Greg was assisted at this point by a team of six expatriates from LCC who were brought in for the short-term training assignment.

Greg had expected that the employees would be very motivated to learn their jobs since their compensation was considerably more than most had previously received in their careers in Russia, and working at a luxury American hotel provided a degree of status. He was disappointed by the responses to the training program. Many of the new employees seemed more interested in asking about compensation, benefits, and how the hotel would benefit them, than specific questions concerning their responsibilities. Greg noticed some of the employees dozing off during the orientation program. In addition, Greg was discouraged by the reactions he received from some of the employees to a gift the hotel gave on the first day of orientation. The hotel provided, as a welcoming gift to each employee, a large basket of toiletries wrapped with a large red ribbon. Some of the employees wanted two or three of the baskets and some asked for money instead. Although this disappointed Greg, many employees appeared grateful for the opportunity to work and seemed motivated to do a good job. Greg was pleased that with the exception of two people, all employees were able to successfully complete their job specific training. With the employees selected and trained, the Ste. Basil Hotel was ready to begin welcoming guests.

A Slow Start

During the first few weeks of operation Greg spent most of his time with external relations. He was busy dealing with suppliers, government officials, and travel industry representatives. Greg delegated much of the day-to-day operations to Victor who would consult with him if a problem arose which he could not handle. Occupancy was very low, as expected, yet the restaurant and café did a brisk business from the start. The low level of occupancy was somewhat beneficial in that it allowed the staff time to continue to learn their duties on-the-job. The American trainers had returned home, and with Greg busy with other matters, Victor made decisions and answered questions from the staff.

Although Greg did not have much contact with many of the employees during this time he did notice that in general the employees did not seem to present the warm, hospitable atmosphere that the hotel sought. The employees infrequently smiled and often seemed to be in a bad mood. Greg mentioned this point to Victor who told him that it was "the Russian nature," but that he would ask the employees to try harder. Greg decided that while he was too busy to intervene, he would try to "catch someone doing it right" and reward him or her with positive reinforcement. On several occasions when he found an employee smiling or presenting the proper attitude he would give them an O.K. sign (thumb and forefinger closed in a circle) as a show of approval. Much to his surprise this provoked a negative reaction in the employees. Greg was also surprised by the frequent use of the Russian word "nyet," in fact, it seemed to Greg that the "no" word was almost an automatic response to any request.

Trouble with Victor

As time went on Greg was able to devote more of his attention to internal operations. He was beginning to become concerned about Victor's approach with employees. While Victor was a handsome and confident man, and appeared to be well liked by the hotel's customers, his approach to employee relations was unattractive. In one particular case a desk clerk was fired in a loud outburst that occurred in front of several guests. It was particularly troubling in that the clerk, Svetlana was a particular favorite of Greg. Svetlana was a divorced mother of two young girls who had been struggling to provide the sole support for her family after her husband left the family. Svetlana was a devout member of the Russian Orthodox Church and Greg considered her to be an honest, conscientious, and faithful employee. Victor informed Greg that he had terminated her for excessive time off. Victor explained that Svetlana had asked for two days off to care for one of her children who was sick and she did not return to work for a week. Victor explained that he had assumed that she had quit, and so he was surprised to see her behind the front desk working. Her attitude was poor according to Victor and she insulted him, and he lost his temper and fired her in front of all parties present. As Greg probed further he was told by Victor that there is an old Russian proverb – "A dog is wiser than a woman. It never barks at its master." It was clear to Greg that Victor had a low opinion of women and that he was engaging in behavior which was inconsistent with LCC company policy. Greg informed Victor that he was going to contact Svetlana and hear her side of the story.

With some difficulty Greg was finally able to contact Svetlana and he asked her to come in to the hotel to discuss the matter. Svetlana told Greg that she did request two days off but that her other child had also become ill and she needed to care for her too. She was fearful to let Victor know that she would not be able to come in for the additional days. Greg was sympathetic and told her that he would reinstate her. When Victor was told of Greg's decision he just shook his head and said "nyekulturny" and walked away. Greg was not sure what this meant but he was sure it wasn't favorable. Greg decided that all decisions concerning employee discipline would first have to be approved by him and he issued a memo stating the policy. Victor took the memo very seriously and proceeded to consult Greg on all personnel matters. He did seem genuine in his actions (although Greg was not completely sure of this) but the constant requests for Greg's approval became a nuisance.

Additional difficulties continued to arise with Victor. It concerned Greg that Victor began spending a lot of time in the hotel restaurant with a small group of Russian men. They didn't appear to ever eat a meal, they only smoked and drank vodka and gave disapproving stares at anyone who came near them. The group appeared to Greg to be a bit rough and not the type of clientele that the hotel sought to attract. After a few weeks Greg decided that it was time to investigate. He began by checking into the amount of money the group was spending in the restaurant and was he shocked to discover that Victor was providing the drinks free of charge to the group. When questioned about this Victor replied that these men were important to the success of the hotel and that the money spent on their drinks was money well spent. Greg was confused by the response and continued to ask about the men. Victor finally stated in a firm tone – "Trust me General Manager, I know what I am doing." Greg felt that he had better let the issue go for now but that he should keep an eye on the situation.

Attempt at Improvement in Customer Service

With the issues concerning Victor still in his mind, Greg decided that he must begin to address the issue of customer service, and he would probably need to do it without Victor's assistance. Although business was beginning to increase, customer feedback was indicated that many guests felt that the hotel staff was not on par with what was expected from a 4-star hotel. Guests commented that the staff was "unhelpful," "uncaring," "cold," and "went out of their way to avoid work." These frequent comments were an embarrassment to Greg and LCC properties so he decided that he should ask for help from the corporate staff to bring the hotel up to standard.

With the arrival of two customer service trainers from the United States an ambitious training program was instituted. Every employee including supervisory staff, would be required to complete 20 hours of additional training. The trainers repeated the initial training in guest relations which the employees had experienced when they were first hired, and additional training was conducted in handling problem guests and seeking continuous improvement in customer relations. An incentive program was designed by the trainers in which each guest would be given a card in which they could recommend an employee for recognition for their good service. At the end of each week the hotel would reward the employee who had accumulated the most recommendations with a certificate for a free meal for two in the hotel restaurant. In addition, the employee would have their picture placed at the front desk with the caption "Employee of the Week." In the next few weeks it did appear that customer service was improving, however, Greg worried that the improvement might be short-lived and that the Ste. Basil would not be able to match the level of service found in other LCC properties. He had heard that some of the employees resented the competitive nature of the incentive.

A Visit by the Krysha

During the following months business improved at the Ste. Basil. As Greg was in his office reviewing the hotel's revenues and expenses for the past six months a smile grew on his face. While there were still problems with customer service, employee punctuality, and employees showing initiative, Greg felt that LCC would be pleased with the operating results of the hotel. The hotel continued to show strong gains in occupancy. The restaurant and café were doing well, but the conference facilities were still underutilized in Greg's opinion. Greg's thoughts were interrupted by a knock on the door. Victor entered and asked if he could speak with him for a moment about a "very important matter." Greg welcomed Victor in and was surprised to see that Victor was not alone. Behind him were four men that Greg had seen previously in the hotel's restaurant with Victor. Greg introduced himself and the men remained silent. Victor seemed very uncomfortable as he explained that the men had requested that the hotel hire them for their services. Greg was not sure what Victor meant, but he was developing an uneasy feeling that something was wrong. Victor explained that the men were needed for "security purposes." Greg realized that Victor did not mean to imply that they were asking for security guard positions and so he asked that the men please step outside the office for a moment. As they did Victor began to explain that the men were members of the Russian mafia and that they wanted protection money. Victor explained that it was quite common in Russia to pay for such a service, but Greg was adamant in his refusal to pay. Greg berated Victor for even bringing the men into his office and questioned why he was meeting with them in the hotel restaurant. Victor stated that he was protecting Greg and the hotel from problems, and that Greg should consider the fact that an American was recently murdered in Moscow by the Russian mafia. Greg told Victor to leave the office and to inform the men that the Ste. Basil did not need their services.

The Russian Cold

As Victor left the office the Greg's telephone rang. It was Dmitry Puzankov, attorney for the Russian partners. Dmitry explained to Greg that the partners wanted to meet with him to discuss some contract matters. When pressed for an explanation Dmitry explained that the partners wanted to renegotiate the profit distribution of the agreement and some "other changes" including their request that Victor be made "Executive General Manager." Upon ending the conversation with Dmitry, Greg telephoned down to the front desk as he wanted to meet with Svetlana and he knew that she was scheduled to be working. Greg had come to rely on Svetlana for advice on Russian culture. He was informed that Svetlana had not reported to work due to the illness of one of her children. As Greg watched the snow fall upon the Moscow streets below he wondered about the security of his present position, the personal safety of himself and his wife, and his future with LCC Properties. It seemed to Greg that the temperature of his office had suddenly dropped as a cold chill ran throughout his body.

SOURCES

Crane, R. (2000). <u>European Business Culture</u>. Harlow, England: Financial Times/Prentice Hall.

Fader, K. (1998). <u>Russia</u>. San Diego, CA: Lucent Books.

Gesteland, R. (1999). <u>Cross-Cultural Business Behavior</u>. Copenhagen: Copenhagen Business School Press.

Mitchell, C. (1998). <u>Passport Russia</u>. San Rafael, CA: World Trade Press.

Morrison, T., Conaway W., and G. Borden. (1994). <u>Kiss, Bow, or Shake Hands</u>. Holbrook, MA: Adams Media.

Munro, R. (2002). *Moscow's Top Hotels Greet the Good Times*. <u>The Moscow Times</u>, May 21.

Newman, P. (1997). *Economic Terrorism in a Moscow Hotel*. <u>Macleans</u>, October 27.

Sears, W. and A. Tamulionyte-Lentz. (2001). <u>Succeeding in Central and Eastern Europe</u>.Woburn, MA: Butterworth-Heinemann.

Smith, B. (1994). <u>The Collaspe of the Soviet Union</u>. San Diego, CA: Lucent Press.

Torchinsky, O. (1997). <u>Cultures of the World: Russia</u>. New York: Marshall Cavendish.

This case was prepared by Charles A. Rarick

CASE 17

AMERITECH IN THE PHILIPPINES

ABSTRACT

An American computer supply company moves its operations to the Philippines in an effort to be more cost competitive but experiences cultural shock as it attempts to institute greater efficiency. The case details the struggles of the plant manager, William Dawson, as he learns the challenges of managing the "Filipino way." The case includes issues such as pakikisama, face saving, and collectivist behavior.

Introduction

AmeriTech was started in Lexington, Kentucky by a small group of former IBM employees who accepted a buyout package offered by the company when the Lexington division was reorganized in 1991. Originally, AmeriTech produced computer supplies such as ink cartages, cables, and other small computer supplies in a facility in North Carolina. The operation proved successful as the demand for such products rose globally, however, over time AmeriTech found itself less competitive in terms of cost over rivals from a number of Asian countries. In an effort to reduce labor costs, the founders moved their operations to Mactan Island near the city of Cebu in the Philippines. Instead of starting a Greenfield operation, AmeriTech was able to purchase an underperforming Korean firm that was operating in the economic zone of the island. AmeriTech purchased the facility and retained the entire workforce of the former Korean owned business. AmeriTech had hoped to continue its efficient and quality-oriented production techniques from North Carolina in the low wage environment of the Philippines.

The Philippines

The Republic of the Philippines is a country in Southeast Asia consisting of over 7,000 islands. The capital is Manila, located on the island of Luzon. The Philippines was "discovered" by Ferdinand Magellan in 1521, who claimed the islands for Spain. The country was named after the Spanish King Philip (Felipe) and missionaries converted most of the population to Catholicism. The Philippines is unique in being the only Christian country in Asia. While Magellan met his death soon after arriving in the Philippines, the country was under Spanish control for a number of years. The Philippines came under the rule of the United States in 1898, when Admiral Dewey defeated the Spanish, and Spain ceded the islands under the Treaty of Paris. While Tagalog, or Filipino is the official language of the Philippines, English is widely spoken, especially among educated Filipinos.

In 1935 the Philippines became a self-governing commonwealth, and there continued to be a strong push by the Filipinos for complete independence. This independence movement was interrupted by World War II when the Japanese invaded the country. With the help of the American forces, the Filipinos defeated the Japanese and gained their independence in 1946. After a number of different administrations, strongman Ferdinand Marcos ruled the country for a number of years and maintained strong ties with the United States. With increasing discontentment of the Filipino people, a "peoples revolution" occurred and Marcos was forced to leave the country. Political instability resulted for a time, however, democracy quickly retook a firm hold in the Philippines. Fidel Ramos became president of the Philippines in 1992, and he opened the economy to market forces and encouraged foreign investment, including the establishment of export processing zones (EPZ) and incentives for foreign firms to establish a presence in the Philippines.

AmeriTech in the Philippines

With an increasing wage rate in North Carolina and the incentives offered by the Philippines, AmeriTech made the decision to close its American facility and begin operating in the Mactan Economic Zone of the Philippines. The area is in the part of the Philippines called the Visayas. With a compatible operating facility being offered for sale, AmeriTech relocated with the hope of gaining a competitive advantage with lower labor costs and access to the emerging markets of Asia. The only employee from North Carolina that would be making the move to the Philippines was William "Bill" Dawson. Dawson was the son of a tobacco farmer in North Carolina, who while deemed by his teachers and peers to be highly intelligent, never attended college. He worked in a number of manufacturing jobs after high school, and through hard work and ability, gained a number of supervisory positions. He was hired by AmeriTech when the firm first began operating in North Carolina as a first line supervisor. Through an unusual series of personnel turnover and one death, he was promoted to plant manager in a few years after first being hired. Dawson instituted a number of quality improvement and inventory management techniques and gained the respect of his superiors. While Bill could be intimidating to some (he was a large, and somewhat heavy man, with a loud voice), he was generally well liked and respected by the employees at AmeriTech. Bill was known for being "firm, but fair." He was very informal with his employees and dressed in a casual, or some would say "sloppy" fashion. The employees appreciated the fact that he was just a "regular guy." Bill was looking forward to his new assignment, however, he feared he would miss watching his beloved North Carolina Tar Heels play basketball on television. While he had never been to the Philippines, he did have a favorable impression of the country from the stories his uncle, who served in World War II, had told him about the Philippines, and the courage of the Filipino fighters. Bill also learned that basketball is a favored sport in the Philippines and so "maybe the place wouldn't be so bad after all."

With an unusually easy transition, AmeriTech took control of the former Korean facility. While adjustments had to be made in the production process, and many of the workers could not be used during this time, AmeriTech generated goodwill by paying the employees their normal salaries during this startup period. The employees that were needed to work were paid their normal salaries plus a 50% bonus during this time. AmeriTech realized that there were going to be additional costs during the startup, including increased training in the "AmeriTech way." In general the employees welcomed the new owners, and many commented that they much preferred working for an American company than a Korean one. One new hire was Miguel Santos, a 26 year old MBA graduate of De la Salle University in Manila. Miguel was hired as an assistant to Bill, and someone to help Bill with any cultural difficulties he might experience in his assignment.

Tensions Begin

Miguel was born and raised in Manila and did not consider himself to be a Cebuano (someone from Cebu or the surrounding area). The employees in the plant were mostly Cebuanos and were at time untrusting of people from Metro Manila. They felt that they were too urban, too serious, and too self-centered for their tastes. Miguel was very deferential to Bill Dawson, refusing to call him by his first name and always referring to him as "Mr. Dawson," and sometimes, "Plant Manager Dawson." Miguel was not as cordial with the lower level employees at the plant, however, and at time had strained relations with employees. Miguel also was not very happy with the fact that he had to leave his family in Manila, and because of the distance, only see them every few months.

The productivity level of the plant remained low for a number of months and Bill had decided that it was time for a change. While he had expected that it might take some time for productivity to reach the levels achieved in North Carolina, he was beginning to feel as if without some intervention, things would not improve. Of particular concern to Bill was the amount of "wasted time" he observed in the plant. Employees would often take extended breaks, chat endlessly among themselves, and often engage in non-work activities while on company time, such as celebrating an employee's birthday. Miguel explained to Bill that it represented "pakikisama" and was quite common in Filipino culture. Bill seemed unconvinced, but proceeded with caution and allowed this to situation to continue, as he was in a phase of "employee relations building" with the employees. After a few more months productivity still had not improved, and Bill decided it was time to take action.

In North Carolina, Bill had learned that when employees were "schooled" in the ways of productivity, they improved their performance. The North Carolina plant also had an individual incentive plan which acted as a strong motivator. Bill reasoned that he should now begin to change the corporate culture of the plant. With the help of Miguel, he organized after-work training sessions and stressed the importance of reducing "wasted time" on the job. Most of the employees were females and many had not worked previously in a manufacturing environment. The training sessions were a bit frustrating to Bill as he could not get the employees to participate nor contribute their thoughts. He felt that if he allowed for employee input, he could win over the employees to his ideas for productivity improvement. The only employee who spoke frequently was a middle aged woman named Millet, who often joked and teased Bill during the training sessions. Bill had gotten the impression that Millet was romantically interested in him, and he was unhappy with the situation. After yet another training session in which little was achieved, so Bill thought, except the asking of personal questions from Millet, Bill decided to have her fired. He instructed Miguel to terminate her employment immediately. Miguel warned Bill that Millet was a productive employee who had worked for the previous company for many years, and that she was very well liked by her peers. Bill responded that he was tired of her teasing and personal questions and that "it was nobody's damn business if he is married or not." Miguel did as he was told and informed Millet she would not be returning to work tomorrow.

The mood of the employees, especially those in Millet's department, changed almost immediately. While it was common to hear cheery voices and laughter in the plant, in the days and weeks that followed, the plant was void of much humor. Employees seemed to be more formal and less warm to Bill, however, there was a slight improvement in productivity. This made Bill happy. He thought that, just maybe, he needed to use a firmer hand in dealing with the workers. He was a bit concerned that employee turnover had increased, but he reasoned that it was probably just employees who did not want to really work. Bill turned his thoughts to ways to introduce a monetary incentive program and to start a quality improvement program.

While Bill pondered such issues, Miguel informed him that another industrial plant was opening in Mactan and that he feared that AmeriTech might lose more employees. Bill was unconcerned, but finally agreed with Miguel that he would call a meeting and announce the incentive program he had been developing. The meeting was scheduled after work hours, and a number of employees did not attend. This angered Bill and he expressed his displeasure by calling out the names of the employees who were not present. He suggested to the gathered employees that maybe those missing employees would not be returning to work next week. The meeting went on, with the rather complex incentive program being explained. The basic idea was that employees would no longer be "entitled" to a salary, but that they could, if properly motivated, earn more money. Within a week, close to 20% of the workforce resigned.

Time for Change, Again

With turnover becoming a problem, and the resulting disruption to production, Bill was under fire from his superiors to turn the situation around. Bill decided to have yet another meeting with his employees, but this time to pay them for attending. Bill expected 100% turnout for the meeting but instead, roughly half the employees attended. Bill was outraged and proceeded to lecture the employees present that the work culture of the company must change. After a very tense 10 minutes of hearing this, Miguel politely interrupted Bill with the suggestion that a break be taken and food delivered to the plant for the employees. This suggestion was not well received by Bill, who then proceeded to criticize Miguel for not understanding the importance of profitability. The meeting ended with a somber mood, as it had begun, and employees quietly left for home. Miguel was one of the first employees to leave the building.

The following day Miguel called in sick, complaining of stomach troubles. Bill decided that maybe he had been too hard on Miguel and the other employees. As he sat at his desk wondering how to proceed, the assistant director of human resources called him to tell him that the director of HR had resigned, for "medical reasons." The department had been busy attempting to fill the vacancies created by the turnover and Bill worried that he was losing the respect of his employees. Bill decided to host an event for all employees in nearby Cebu City, honoring the most dedicated and outstanding employees. When Miguel returned to work the following day, Bill informed him of his decision. Miguel seemed less than excited about the idea. When pressed for an explanation, Miguel admitted that a party was maybe a good idea, but that he, Bill, should not take a very active role in the event. Surprised by this recommendation, Bill pressed Miguel for answers. After much pressuring Miguel blurted out that the employees had a nickname for him – "baboy." Bill was told it meant pig in Tagalog. With this revelation Bill decided to cancel any plans for a party and to resume his normal style of management. He instructed Miguel to begin looking for a new HR director and to ramp up the recruitment of employee replacements.

This case was prepared by Charles A. Rarick, Arifin Angriawan, and Inge Nickerson.

Case previously published in the Journal of the International Academy for Case Studies, 6(1), 2010.

EXERCISE 8

WHICH EXPATRIATE TO CHOSE?

Purpose: The purpose of this exercise is to explore skills and abilities useful for expatriate success.

Procedure: Read the job background note and the candidate bios that follow. Assemble into groups and discuss the qualifications of each candidate as they relate to the position. Select the candidate that you feel would make the best choice for the international assignment. Also answer the two questions which follow the employee bios.

Position Background:

Ozarks Fine Furniture, an American company has recently acquired a furniture manufacturer located in a city outside Bucharest, Romania. Ozarks hope to be able to eventually shift some of its more labor-intensive manufacturing to this new plant. The company is planning on sending one of its employees to Romania for a period of three years to oversee the operation and to make recommendations. The selected employee would be given the title of Executive Director and will be the highest ranking employee in the Romanian company. Three employees have expressed an interest in the position.

Employee Bios:

Jim Watson: Jim has been with Ozarks since graduating with a B.S. degree in business administration from the College of the Ozarks. He is currently Vice President of Manufacturing, having risen up the organizational structure. Jim is a highly rated employee. He is viewed as conscientious, hard working, and fair-minded. His performance reviews have always been outstanding Jim is generally seen as a likable and easy-going person. He is 27 years old and married to an elementary school teacher. The Watson's have one child, age two. Jim enjoys hunting, fishing, coaching Little League baseball, reading, and motorcycles. He speaks only English and has traveled internationally to Canada, Mexico, Jamaica, and England.

Sarah Smith: Sarah has been employed with Ozarks for two years as the Director of Marketing. She reports directly to the CEO of Ozarks and is considered to be a highly intelligent and competent employee. Sarah has an M.B.A. from the University of Arkansas and has previous work experience in advertising and sales. She is seen by her fellow employees as being a nice person, but a perfectionist. Her performance as marketing director has been outstanding. Sarah is 32 years old and married with two children, ages seven and five. Her husband is the owner of a web-based publishing company. She enjoys crafts, computers, skiing, and basketball. Sarah speaks English, French, and Spanish and has traveled internationally to Canada, Mexico, Costa Rica, Venezuela, Chile, Argentina, France, Ireland, and England.

Gus Dinu: Gus has been a production supervisor at Ozarks for the past 12 years. He began with Ozarks on the assembly line and has previous experience in auto repair. Gus, age 48, came to the United States as a teenager when his family emigrated from Romania. He speaks English and Romanian, and some Russian. Gus enjoys hunting, fishing, and auto restoration. He is married, with two children, ages nineteen and twenty two. His wife is currently unemployed but worked previously as a receptionist. Gus is a hard working and effective supervisor, although some of his employees view him as too inflexible and moody. His performance reviews are generally very good. Gus has traveled internationally to Romania and France.

What additional information about the candidates might be useful?

What questions would you ask each candidate, if you were interviewing them for the assignment?

EXERCISE 9

DESIGNING A COMPENSATION PACKAGE

Purpose: The purpose of this exercise is to gain familiarity with the challenges of designing an effective compensation program for an international assignment.

Procedure: Read the background information below, research the country to which the expatriate will be sent, and design what you consider an equitable compensation package.

Background Information:

Jack Simon, a middle manager for a medium-sized American firm is being sent to Brussels for a three-year assignment. Jack will be moving with his wife and three children, ages eleven, fourteen, and sixteen. Jack lives in Cincinnati, Ohio with his family in a four-bedroom house and currently earns $102,500. In addition to his salary, Jack receives a number of benefits including health insurance for the entire family. In Belgium Jack will be paid his salary in euros.

The HR department of Jack's company is attempting to develop a compensation package which will fairly compensate Jack during his three years in Brussels. An investigation into international assignment compensation has uncovered issues such as foreign service premium, educational allowances, hardship allowances, housing allowances, and tax equalization. The department is seeking your advice (be specific) on how Jack should be compensated.

PART FIVE

SOCIAL RESPONSIBILITY

We have seen the important impact of culture on international business and management. Culture also influences organizational behavior relative to ethics and corporate social responsibility. Two basic ethical orientations found globally are a universal and relative approach. The universal approach assumes that ethical behavior should not vary from country to country. The relativist approach proposes that what is right or wrong varies based on culture, economic development, and other variables. The following cases describe some country differences in ethical values, legal, and social responsibility. Consecutively, the cases describe slavery practices in the international chocolate industry, the issues of environmental protection, and corruption and bribery.

Cases:
Child Slavery and the Chocolate Industry
Drilling for Riches in the Rainforest
Stew Morrison's Business Trip to Nigeria

Exercise:
Are Ethical Principles Universal?

CASE 18

CHILD SLAVERY IN THE INTERNATIONAL CHOCOLATE INDUSTRY

ABSTRACT

This case explores the modern day practice of child slavery in the West African country of Cote D'Ivoire. Children as young as eight years old are forced into slavery from other West African countries to work in the harvesting of cocoa beans which are purchased by American and European MNC's for the production of chocolate. The case examines the political, social, and economic forces which impact child slavery in West Africa and allows for discussion of possible solutions to this troubling situation.

Siaka is from Mali, a poor West African country which supplies much of the labor used to harvest cocoa beans grown in Cote D'Ivoire (Ivory Coast) and exported to many countries including the United States. Cocoa is used in the production of chocolate and the heavy demand for chocolate products throughout the world keeps Siaka and his peers busy. The cocoa bean harvesters work long hours; in most cases they work during all available daylight time in the hot African sun. In addition to the work being very demanding, Siaka is only 14 years old and he is a slave of the cocoa bean plantation.

Cote d'Ivoire

Located in West Africa, the Ivory Coast, or more formally, the Republique de Cote d'Ivoire was known by Europeans as a trading area for ivory. Named by French sailors, the area was dominated by the French and Portuguese in the sixteenth and seventeenth centuries. Early contact

Charles Rarick and Arifin Angriawan

with the people of the area by Europeans involved the trading of ivory, gold, and later slaves. Because of the advantages of neighboring countries such as present day Ghana which had a better harbor, Cote d'Ivoire was saved from much trafficking in slaves. In the 1840's the French began negotiating with local tribal leaders and established a military outpost, and by 1893 Cote d'Ivoire became a colony of the French government. The French built plantations and engaged in forced labor on these plantations. In 1944 a tribal chief named Houphouet-Boigng established a trade union of African farmers which eventually became a political party known as the Democratic Party of Cote d'Ivoire. After struggling for independence, the country finally became free of French rule in 1960 and Houphouet-Boigng became Cote d'Ivoire's first president.

With a growing economy based on agriculture and a continuing rise in the standard of living of most citizens, the country remained politically stable until the 1980's. As commodity prices dropped, political tensions mounted. Cote d'Ivoire was an independent country, but a country with only one political party, and a press controlled by the government. After violent protests Houphouet-Boigng agreed to allow for a free press and additional political parties. Even with competing political parties and leaders, Houphouet-Boigng remained as president of the country until his death in 1993. Cote d'Ivoire remained a democracy until 1999 when a coup d'etat lead by General Robert Guei overthrew the elected government and took power. Elections were held in 2000 but were tainted when Guei stopped the counting of ballots and declared himself the winner. Riots broke out and Guei was forced to leave the country. His opponent, Laurent Gbagbo then became president.

Cote d'Ivoire remains politically unstable and economically disadvantaged. The country ranks 77th out of the 91 countries Transparency International lists in its corruption index. Like Cote d'Ivoire, many African countries rank towards the bottom of the scale, indicating significant corruption. The economy is heavily dependent of agricultural prices which can fluctuate significantly. Seventy percent of the population earns its living in agriculture and the country relies of the export of cocoa, bananas, palm oil, rice and timber to sustain itself. Light manufacturing such as food processing and textiles provide few jobs. The economy is especially linked to the market price of cocoa in that Cote d'Ivoire is the world's largest producer of this commodity. The social structure is divided along religious, tribal, and geographical lines. Sixty-percent of the population is Muslim, 12% Christian, and 18% follow various indigenous religions. Cote d'Ivoire consists of a number of distant tribes, each with its own identity, and in some cases language. Compared to some neighboring countries Cote d'Ivoire has a more prosperous economy, however, per capita GDP is still only $1600. Life expectancy is 47 years and Cote d'Ivoire ranks 154th out of 171 countries in the Human Development Index. Cote d'Ivoire is a poor nation, however, two of its neighbors are even poorer and the reason that the children from these countries are brought into Cote d'Ivoire as slaves. Mali and Bukina Faso, two countries to the north have GDP's per capita of $800 and $1,100, respectively.

Slavery, Past and Present

Slavery in Africa has a long history and began long before the Europeans arrived to export slaves to New World for work on plantations. The early African empires that developed thousands of years ago often engaged in battle among themselves. The winning kingdoms often took prisoners and made slaves of the defeated people. These early slaves were required to do undesirable tasks or to become soldiers and fight for the conquering kingdom. When trade routes developed across the Sahara, slaves became a commodity to be traded. With the arrivals of Europeans, slaves began to be exported from Africa. Local rulers traded captured slaves and even began to hunt slaves for additional export. The slave trade was very lucrative for the local kings. Major slave trading was conducted from West Africa, from which millions of Africans were sent to America and the Caribbean between the fifteenth and nineteenth centuries.

Most people assume that slavery is just an unpleasant memory from the distant past. The idea that slavery still exists in the world is difficult to believe but it, nevertheless, is true. Modern slavery comes in a variety of forms including bonded labor, forced labor, forced marriage servitude, and chattel slavery. Bonded labor involves obtaining a loan and then agreeing to work in order to pay off the loan. Often the borrower is held against his/ her will, forced to work long hours, and may never be able to pay off the loan because the lender charges for food, shelter and other expenses. Forced labor slaves are taken by governments or individuals and made to work against their will under the threat of violence or death. Forced marriage servitude involves the marriage of usually young women against their will and the imposed duties of working without choice for the husband and/or his extended family. Chattel slavery is the more traditional form of slavery in which people are bought and sold as property. The children of West Africa who are harvesting cocoa beans in Cote d'Ivoire more typically fall into the forced labor form of slavery. These young boys are recruited to work in Cote d'Ivoire with the promise of good wages and often some form of valuable training. They are instead then forced to work long hours with no pay and are often beaten by their masters. The families of the children are sometimes given a "gesture of respect" or small payment for their children and the payment can be as low as $1.50US. The farmers on the cocoa farms promise to pay the children at the end of the year, assuming the price of cocoa is sufficiently high enough, however, seldom do the children receive any payments for their work.

A number of international agreements prohibit slavery, such as the 1948 Universal Declaration of Human Rights and the 1956 United Nations Supplementary Convention on the Abolition of Slavery. However, few African countries do much to abide by the agreements. Only Ghana, Togo, and Senegal have signed the 1999 International Labour Council convention which requires countries to take action to halt child slavery. In West and Central Africa girls as young as eight years old work as domestics, and in Tanzania girls less than fifteen work as prostitutes in nightclubs. Only recently has anyone ever been convicted of child trafficking in Cote d'Ivoire. In 2001, for the first time, four people were arrested for trafficking in child slaves. They were jailed for two months and fined the US equivalent of $67. UNICEF estimates that as many as 200,000 children are sold into slavery each year in Africa. Although slavery and the trafficking of slaves are illegal, it is often difficult to enforce, and enforcement is hampered by a general acceptance of the long standing practice. Many of the cocoa farms are in remote areas of Cote d'Ivoire and the legal working age of 14 is seldom enforced in the country. Child slaves often work along side the children of farm owners making it difficult for investigators to identify them. Ignorance of the laws, corrupt law enforcement, and a lack of resources also keep the slavery trade in business.

The Lost Boys

The children who work the cocoa farms are desperate for work in order to supplement their family's incomes. It is not uncommon for the men of the area to have multiple wives and many children. It becomes necessary for the children to work in order to supplement family income. A "locateur" is a slave trader. The locateur finds the boys, generally aged 12-16, who will be enticed to leave home in the hope of earning money for their families and learning a trade. The locateurs sometimes entice the boys with promises of getting a new bicycle. The locateur is also responsible for smuggling the boys across the border and finding a farmer who will pay for the boys. Since it illegal for a child to cross the border into Cote d'Ivoire without a relative, the locateur often instructs the boys to call him "uncle." Some boys are routed into the country through the back roads in order to avoid suspicion.

Once on the farms the boys learn quickly that the promises made by the locateurs are false. They work without pay in the blistering African sun and are locked in small huts for the night. Sometimes the boys may be paid at the end of the year if the price of cocoa is high, however, the price of cocoa had dropped from a high of $4.89 a pound in 1977 to about $0.50 today. Most boys never receive pay for their work. Their identification is confiscated by their masters and they live on very little food – usually just corn paste and bananas. If they try to escape they will be beaten. The job of a cocoa slave is to cut pods from a cacao tree, split open the pod and scoop out the beans and place them in the sun to dry. It takes approximately 400 cocoa beans to make a pound of chocolate. The beans are collected from different farms and sold as a commodity to processors such as ADM of the United States. Eventually the cocoa is processed into chocolate products by companies such as Hershey Foods, Mars, Nestle, and Russell Stover Candies. Countries which are big consumers of Cote d'Ivoire cocoa are the United States, Germany, and the United Kingdom. The boys of the cocoa farms do eventually earn their freedom, but they leave the farms broken physically, and psychologically.

Industry and Government Response

The government of Cote d'Ivoire initially denied the existence of child slaves on the cocoa farms, but later admitted that some indentured child labor was being used. Some in the government argue that the reason children are being used in this manner is that the price of cocoa has dropped to the point that farmers cannot afford to pay anyone to harvest the beans. They contend that when the price of cocoa rises, the farmers will be able to pay their workers and will not use slave labor. Public pressure has caused the government of Cote d'Ivoire to crack down on children coming over the border to work and has begun to make some arrests of slave traffickers.

Blame for child slave labor in Cote d'Ivoire is deflected by all parties involved. The government blames the low price of cocoa and foreigners who bring the children into the country. Cocoa farmers deny not paying the children and also blame the price of cocoa for causing them to delay payment for labor. Slave traders argue that they do not know that the farmers are not paying the children for their services. The cocoa buyers contend that they have not seen child slaves and that the problem, is in the worst case, simply overblown. As one cocoa buyer states: "You damn Americans with your Nike shoes think there is child slavery in chocolate. I have never seen any child slaves in all my travels through Africa." Cocoa processors complain that it impossible to differentiate cocoa harvested on slave farms from cocoa that is harvested by hired workers. The cocoa beans get mixed together and there is no way of sorting out free cocoa from slave cocoa.

Chocolate manufacturers are aware of the problem, and many have condemned the practices of child slavery. The industry has commissioned a study of the cocoa harvesting practices on Cote d'Ivoire farms. The study will include 2,000 farms in Cote d'Ivoire and also 1,000 farms in Ghana. The research team will attempt to determine the severity of the problem and find possible solutions to the problem. The industry has avoided a boycott of Cote d'Ivoire cocoa due to fears that such a boycott may make the situation worse, in that farmers will be motivated to use more slaves to work the farms due to the lower market price of Cote d'Ivoire cocoa. The Chocolate Manufacturers Association has hired former senators Bob Dole and George Mitchell to lobby Congress against a proposed "slave free" label requirement on chocolate products. The United States Congress began debating legislation which would require chocolate manufacturers to label their products if they contained cocoa from Cote d'Ivoire. Supporters of the requirement feel that this would make consumers aware of the child slavery issue and force chocolate manufacturers to bring pressure on the Cote d'Ivoire government to ban the practice.

While Congress debates the merits of a labeling requirement and the chocolate industry conducts its study, the slave children of West Africa continue to work long hours to produce the ingredients needed for consumers to enjoy their favorite chocolate products.

SOURCES

Anonymous. (2001). *Child Slavery a Multibillion-Dollar Industry Targeting Africa*. African News Service, June 5.
Chatterjee, S. (2001). *Chocolate Companies Air Their Comments on Slavery in Ivory Coast*. Knight-Ridder/Tribune Business News, June 25.

Chatterjee, S. (2001). *Nearly Hidden, Slavery on the Ivory Coast Cocoa Farms is Easy to Miss.* Knight-Ridder/Tribune Business News, June 25.

Chatterjee, S. (2001). *Chocolate Makers Fight Slave Free Label.* Miami Herald, August 1.

Kummer, P. (1996). Cote d'Ivoire. NY: Grolier Publishing.

McCuen, G. (1998). Modern Slavery and the Global Economy. Hudson, WI: GEM Publications.

Raghavan, S. and S. Chatterjee. (2001). *Chocolate's Sweetness Tainted by Slavery.* Miami Herald, June 24.

Raghavan, S. (2001). *Village Elders, Foreigners Work to Free Children.* Miami Herald, June 25.

Raghavan, S. (2001). *Ivory Coast Accused of Detaining Hundreds of School-Aged Boys.* Miami Herald, June 28.

Romei, S. (2001). *Slavery's Bitter Chocolate.* The Australian, April 24.

Sankoh, O. (2001). *Child Slavery: A Case for Juliet and Janet.* African News Service, June 19.

Sheehan, P. (2000). Cultures of the World: Cote d'Ivoire. Tarrytown, NY: Marshall Cavendish Publishing.

Sheehan, S. (1999). The Great African Kingdoms. Austin, TX: Raintree Steck-Vaughn Publishers.

WWW.Antislavery.org

WWW.Countrywatch.com

WWW.Hersheys.com

WWW.State.gov

Zavis, A. (2001). *Africa's Youth Harvest Misery.* Los Angeles Times, May 13.

This case was prepared by Charles A. Rarick and previously published in the Journal of the American Academy of Business, 2002.

CASE 19

DRILLING FOR RICHES IN THE RAIN FOREST

ABSTRACT

The new CEO of a major oil company is faced with a difficult decision. His company is being sued in a South American court for billions of dollars based on the claim of environmental harm caused by its drilling operations. The company has, up to this point, proclaimed its innocence and blamed the damage on its local partner. The new CEO must decide if the company's action was ethical and what action, if any, he should take now.

Brandon McClelland became the CEO of Texas-Champion only a month ago. The Houston-based oil company was created by the merger of two Texas oil companies. McClelland has faced a number of challenges in his short tenure as CEO, but his biggest challenge has been what to do about a looming trial in which his company has been named as a defendant. Texas-Champion is being sued by a group of Ecuadorian residents for damage they claim was caused by the company when it operated in a remote part of Ecuador.

Texas Oil Holdings in Ecuador

In 1964, Texas Oil Holdings entered into a joint venture with the Ecuadorian oil company, Petroecuador, to explore and drill for oil in the Ecuadorian Amazon. After the agreement ended in 1992, Texas oil pulled out of Ecuador and left the operation to Petroecuador, as had been previously agreed. Shortly after Texas Oil left Ecuador, a group of indigenous people living near the site of its oil operations brought a lawsuit in the United States charging Texas Oil with environmental damage. The suit claimed that Texas Oil was careless in its operations, allowing contaminated water to enter the water system of the area and leaving behind hundreds of pools of oil. The area is environmentally sensitive and the plaintiffs claim that great harm has occurred to their land, and they are experiencing health problems as a result of the contamination. Texas Oil defended itself claiming that it followed all environmental laws in Ecuador, and that it was only a minority shareholder in the joint venture. Texas Oil contended that if anyone were responsible for environmental damage in Ecuador, it would be Petroecudaor.

The lawsuit brought in the United States was dismissed on the basis that the appropriate jurisdiction was not the United States, but Ecuador. The case was refiled in Ecuador, with estimated damages of between $1.6 and $6.15 billion. Texas-Champion has claimed that it is not responsible for any damage to the environment because the company no longer exists. Texas Oil Holdings merged with Champion Oil in 2002 and the old company, Texas Oil Holdings, was dissolved. The new company, Texas-Champion is a completely separate legal entity. The company also countered that it paid $40 million in 1998 to clean up the area, and that its payment relieved the company of all liability.

Reviewing the Arguments

In his office in Houston, Mr. McClelland reviews a number of files the company has maintained on the case. He reads the charges the Ecuadorians have brought against his company and the responses the company has relative to those charges. He reviews the many legal documents and medical reports in the files.

The plaintiffs are maintaining that Texas dumped millions of gallons of toxic wastewater in the rainforest. The company maintains that it followed acceptable industry practices at the time, and that all of its actions were approved by the Ecuadorian government. The Minister of Energy for Ecuador stated in a court deposition "the government trusted Texas to do the right thing, and we lacked environmental engineers to know what should have been done." When Texas drilled for oil, water trapped below the earth's surface came up with the oil. A separation process was used and the water was discharged into local rivers and streams. The company contends that this process is still used today in many parts of the world including Mexico, Colombia, Indonesia, and Nigeria.

Local residents in the El Oriente region, the area of contamination, claim that they no longer are able to grow crops because of the pollution. Most crops will not grow at all, and the few that do, produce a poor harvest. Mr. McClelland read the testimony of farmers who had planted plantain crops which previously grew in abundance in the region and now only produce small fruit, if any at all. He feels empathy for these farmers, especially since he grew up on a farm in western Texas, and as a boy watched his father try to grow crops in an often inhospitable growing environment. Mr. McClelland also reads the files that indicate that the residents of El Oriente have suffered from an unusually high rate of medical conditions such as cancer. A report, prepared by a doctoral student doing his dissertation on the medical conditions of the region, showed a statistically significant difference in the health problems of the people in the region. Another report contained in the file, this one commissioned by the company, showed that previous medical studies were flawed and inadequate. This report cautioned readers from drawing conclusions without a comparative study based on people with similar diet and regular medical care.

The files Mr. McClelland has in his possession also include pictures of many open oil pits, many of them near local resident's homes. People living in the area complain about the smell which comes from the open pits. As he reviews the photos, Mr. McClelland is confused as to why this environmental damage is still present. After Texas Oil paid $40 million for a cleanup of the region, the Ecuadorian government declared the area rehabilitated.

As he looks over all the documentation of the case, Mr. McClelland thinks about the upcoming trial in Ecuador. He has been told that the case will be heard in the small town of Largo Agrio, in a courtroom that by American standards would be considered quite primitive. He also wonders about a potential jury that will be selected from the area's residents. As he ponders all the facts, including the faces of the indigenous people in the pictures, he wonders what his responsibilities are in this situation. Mr. McClelland concludes that some of the presented facts are true. He believes that significant environmental damage has occurred in the region and that damage is still present. He believes that the local residents are being adversely affected by the environmental damage, and he believes that Texas Oil Holdings had a responsibility to avoid significant environmental damage as it operated in the rainforest. What he is not sure of is the responsibility of Texas-Champion at this point, given the fact that the company paid the agreed upon settlement for the damage, and the fact that Texas Oil Holdings no longer exists.

This case is a fictional account of an actual situation involving an American oil company operating in Ecuador. The case was prepared by Charles A. Rarick.

CASE 20

STEW MORRISON'S BUSINESS TRIP TO NIGERIA

ABSTRACT

On his first business trip to Africa, Stew Morrison discovers that sometimes opportunity comes with a cost. The great opportunity he had hoped to capitalize on appeared to offer little in the way of rewards. The case explores the issue of corruption and bribery and poses questions relative to the legality of certain actions.

Sitting at the desk in his office in Atlanta, Stew Morrison was elated by the contents of an envelope that had recently arrived from Africa. The envelope contained a letter and supporting documentation from a contact Stew had established in Nigeria and was promising to provide many new customers for Stew's company. Stew Morrison was the CEO of a company called, e-Future; a company that specialized in the sale of education vouchers for the developing world. The letter from Nigeria indicated that a number of businesses, and the government of Nigeria were very interested in purchasing the education vouchers. The letter invited Stew to come to Nigeria and meet with these important prospective customers. Stew was confident that the business was finally beginning to turn around and he was excited about the prospects awaiting him in Nigeria.

e-Future

Begun with limited capital from a few wealthy investors in 2002, e-Future was a company with a dream. That dream was to bring education to the developing world. Stew Morrison, a former professor of education, had developed the idea of offering a simple means for potential students to pay for higher education and technical training through the use of electronic vouchers. Individuals could purchase the vouchers themselves, or the vouchers could be purchased by governments for their citizens. It was also assumed that businesses may offer them as incentives to their employees. The vouchers could be used in a number of universities and technical schools in Africa, Asia, and in Latin America. In addition, an on-line university created by e-Future offered a number of courses and would accept the voucher as payment. The voucher concept reduced the cost of a course significantly, as universities and schools deeply discounted their tuition under the program. The business concept, first developed by Morrison found its way to Jay Nettlehouse, who in turn convinced other private investors to fund startup of the organization. Nettlehouse became Chairman of e-Future and continued to provide financial support for the company. While the private investors hoped to profit from the business, they also hoped that their money would be used to help develop the poorer countries of the world. Unfortunately, sales of the vouchers proved to be more difficult than anticipated. The company had yet to make a profit and the private investors had to make additional contributions to keep the business operational.

Nigeria

While Stew had never to been on the African continent, he had no concerns with the upcoming trip to Nigeria. Doing some research Stew learned that Nigeria had gained its independent from Britain in 1960 and that political instability had ensued up until 1999 when a democratic government was established. He discovered that Nigeria is a diverse country with over 250 ethnic groups. The country is divided by religious identity with the north being mostly Muslim and the south being mostly Christian. The political boundaries of present day Nigeria came into being when the British gained control of the area in the late 1800's and established the area as a colony. During World War II, Nigerians fought with the British and shortly thereafter gained some autonomy, and a constitution. Stew learned from his investigations that democracy has not been the norm during Nigeria's short existence. Due to differing religious and ethnic identities, a series of coups and dictators had exercised power during most of Nigeria's history. With democracy once again in place, Stew felt that perhaps e-Future could help Nigeria in its nation building effort. Stew was encouraged by the fact that Nigeria is a leading supplier of crude oil to the world and is the most populated country in Africa with over 90 million inhabitants. Stew also was happy to learn that English was the official language of Nigeria. While Stew felt that Nigeria offered great promise to e-Future, he also had some concerns about the level of corruption found in the country. He had read that corruption was a problem, and that some foreigners had been victims of various scams.

Bimbola

When Stew arrived at the Lagos airport he was overwhelmed by the sights and sounds he was experiencing. The airport was very noisy and crowded and being tired from his long journey, he felt as if he was too confused to find his way past immigration and get his luggage. As he wandered towards the immigration area he saw a sign being held up by a rather small, middle-aged man. The sign read "Welcome Mr. Stew Morrison". When he approached the man with the sign he realized that it was his contact in Nigeria, Bimbola Ogunk. The two men exchanged greetings and Bimbola took Stew's handbag and escorted him towards immigration. When Stew asked Bimbola if he would have any trouble passing through immigration Bimbola told him not to worry. He reminded Stew that he had connections and asked if he had acquired a Nigerian visa. Stew replied that he had not, as previously instructed by Bimbola, and Bimbola said "no problem." The two men proceeded to a separate line at the immigration stop and Bimbola told the official "this is my special friend." The official looked at Stew and waved the two through immigration. To Stew, it did appear that Bimbola had connections. Stew retrieved his luggage and the two men headed for the exit. Bimbola had arranged for Stew to stay at a hotel where he had further connections. Stew at that point just wanted to get to the hotel as quickly as possible and sleep. Unfortunately the traffic of Lagos would keep Stew from his room for another two hours. The two men chatted on the way to the hotel with Bimbola constantly reassuring Stew that he had connection in the government, and connections with education officials, and industry leaders. Stew would be meeting some of those officials later in the week, he was told. Bimbola also told Stew that he wanted to take him on a trip first; a trip he would "surely enjoy." Stew checked into his hotel to get some sleep.

Early the next morning the telephone in the hotel room rang and it was Bimbola. He told Stew that he was in the hotel lobby and ready to take him on a special tour. Stew arranged for a quick breakfast before leaving with Bimbola for a trip to Benin. The long trip, over 200 miles, allowed Stew the opportunity to get to know Bimbola better. The two men discussed many things, however, Bimbola seemed unable or unwilling to provide any details as to how he was going to arrange for the sale of large quantities of e-Future vouchers. He frequently told Stew not to worry and that he, Bimbola, would handle everything. When pressed, Bimbola told Stew that he had arranged for a meeting with Dr. Kema Agaguelu, Minister of Education and that she was very interested in the educational voucher system offered by Stew's company. While not much business was discussed on the trip to Benin, Stew did learn much about the ancient walled city and about the once great kingdom. He was grateful to Bimbola for taking him to see the impressive sights.

Meet Dr. Agaguela

The entire day, and much of the night was taken up by the trip to Benin. Stew was feeling weary and anxious to return to his room for a good night's rest. Although exhausted, he hardly slept due to the differences in time zones. The following morning he awoke to the sound of the telephone ringing. It was Bimbola greeting him good morning. The two ate breakfast in the hotel restaurant and Bimbola explained to Stew that the meeting with Dr. Agaguela was going to take place that day, later in the afternoon. He told Stew that he should get his presentation material together to show the education minister. Bimbola explained that while the government offices were in the capital, Abuja, the Education Minister had an office in Lagos and that it would not be necessary to travel to the capital to meet her.

The traffic in Lagos was horrendous and it took hours to reach the government building. Bimbola escorted Stew up the flights of stairs in the rather stark building to meet the minister. They arrived on the fifth floor and entered an office void of any marking to find a middle-aged woman sitting behind a desk looking at some papers. Bimbola introduced her as the Minister of Education and Stew began to make a presentation on what his company could offer Nigeria. He went into great detail explaining how the government could advance higher education through the e-Future program, all the time Dr. Agaguelu listened and smiled. While she never asked any questions, she seemed very interested in what Stew had told her, and she thanked him for visiting. Bimbola told Stew that he had made a very good impression on her and that she would certainly be recommending that the government purchase a very large quantity of vouchers. Stew felt a bit uneasy about the meeting but he was encouraged by what Bimbola was telling him. Stew began to press Bimbola for more details on other contacts but Bimbola told him not to worry. Bimbola stated that it was time for Stew to purchase some gifts for his family back in America.

Bimbola took Stew to a large market for shopping. While Stew had no interest in shopping at this time, he felt it best not to insult his host. The market was unlike anything Stew had ever seen. A mix of food and household items, along with crafts and animal skins and skulls. The variety and unique nature of the market was overwhelming to Stew. He managed to purchase some craft items and a special type of woven cloth recommended by Bimbola. It was approaching dinnertime and Bimbola told Stew that he had arranged for Stew to meet his family that evening. Bimbola took Stew to a restaurant where Bimbola's wife and many adults were waiting. The group represented Bimbola's immediate family as well as members of his extended family. Although the group was rather large, Stew enjoyed his meal and the company of this quite lively group of people. One of the dinner items Stew especially enjoyed was jollof rice, a Nigerian specialty. He was impressed when told by one of Bimbola's brothers that Bimbola's grandmother had invented the national dish. Some of the previous apprehensions Stew felt about Bimbola were beginning to be eased. When the waiter brought the restaurant bill to Stew, the moment was a bit uneasy. The bill was quite high and he wasn't sure who was expected to pay, but he reasoned that he would pay the bill since Bimbola had been so kind in taking him to Benin as a cultural side trip. The evening ended well and it appeared to Stew that Bimbola's family had enjoyed the meal. Bimbola took Stew back to the hotel and told him to "expect great things tomorrow."

Great Expectations

Once again it was a night without much sleep for Stew. He was dragging during the day and awake most of the night. He hoped that he would be able to soon adjust to the time difference and get a good night's sleep. He was also uneasy because he still was not able to call home and speak to his wife, as the hotel's international telephone line was not working. As the telephone rang in his room, Stew knew that it Bimbola and he was looking forward to those great expectations promised by Bimbola. Bimbola told Stew that he had very good news for him and to come down to the hotel restaurant and they would discuss it. Over breakfast Bimbola had a hard time containing his happiness. He finally told Stew that he had heard from the Minister of Education and that she was arranging for the government of Nigeria to make an initial purchase of $500,000US e-Future education vouchers. Stew was excited about the news and thanked Bimbola for helping to arrange the meeting that produced these results. Bimbola told Stew that all that was needed now were three things. First, Bimbola would need the bank account number of e-Future in order to wire the funds, secondly, Stew would need to make a small payment of $10,000US to the education minister for her help, and lastly, e-Future would need to pay Bimbola a $50,000US finder's fee. Stew was taken aback by these requests. He asked Bimbola to explain more but all that Bimbola would tell him was that this is the way business was conducted in Nigeria. Bimbola told Stew that unless he wanted to lose this large contract, he would need to meet those three conditions. Stew told Bimbola that he was not sure if he would be able to do what was requested and that he would have to check with someone back in Atlanta. Bimbola told Stew that time was critical and that if he waited, he would certainly lose the contact.

Without the matter being resolved, Bimbola proceeded to tell Stew that he was going to meet with very high-level industry officials who were interested in hearing about the education vouchers for use with their companies. They were going to meet for lunch and so Stew needed once again to gather his presentation material and come along for a ride across town. On the drive across town Bimbola explained how many Americans are surprised by the way business is done in Nigeria but that "once they realize this they are able to acquire very good contracts and earn much money." Bimbola told Stew that "Nigeria is a good place to do business."

A Long Lunch

At lunch, Stew met with four men who were introduced by Bimbola as the leaders of Nigeria's business community. One gentleman, Segun Adelaja was introduced as Prince Segun, head of the Nigerian National Petroleum Corporation. Each man gave Stew a business card indicating their association with various business groups in Nigeria. In addition to the oil industry, the men represented textiles, agriculture, and manufacturing. The six men ate lunch and discussed many things including their love of "football" but not much attention was directed towards business, or e-Future's product. Stew felt very tired and his patience was getting thin. He asked to speak to Bimbola alone and expressed his concerns with the lack of business substance. Bimbola explained that in Nigeria it was customary for people to get to know each other first before they discussed business. Bimbola told Stew that he would provide the opportunity for Stew to present his business ideas before the group left. After many hours of entertaining Bimbola finally told the group "Mr. Morrison has a plan that is of great value to each of you." Acting on this cue, Stew proceeded to tell the men how e-Future could help their industries, and Nigeria in general. The men seemed very interested and asked a number of questions. Stew felt encouraged and continued to discuss product features at great length. After more than five hours of eating, drinking, and discussing, Bimbola told the group that Mr. Morrison had to get back to his hotel and that that they should contact him, Bimbola, if they were interested in having their companies buy the vouchers. He told the group that he strongly recommended that they take advantage of this opportunity. Once again Stew was presented with a rather large bill from the restaurant.

Bimbola drove Stew back to his hotel and explained that these men represented the best opportunity for Stew to sell thousands of vouchers. He told Stew that millions of dollars were at stake and that it was necessary that Stew completely trust Bimbola to make the deals. All that would be required was for Stew give Bimbola his normal ten percent fee, along with a retainer of "a few thousand dollars, today." Stew felt as if he was being played by Bimbola and told him that he needed to rest before making any decisions. Stew felt that it was time to make a call to Jay Nettlehouse back in Atlanta. At the hotel Stew once again experienced difficulties making an international call. His frustration level was rising and he was unsure of what he should do. While he was worried that he might be taken advantage of by Bimbola, he didn't want to miss out on the opportunities that may emerge from the relationships Bimbola provided. Stew decided to try and find another way of calling America. Stew sat on his bed watching television, resting, worrying, and wondering what his next move should be.

An Official Contract

When the telephone rang in his room Stew hoped that it would be someone from e-Future calling. It was Bimbola who told Stew that he was coming over to the hotel for dinner and that he was bringing Stew "something that would make him very happy." When pressed as to what the surprise was, Bimbola told him that it was a contract from the Nigerian government. Stew decided to rest a bit before dinner and was hopeful that perhaps something was finally developing.

Bimbola arrived for dinner with Stew and brought along Dr. Agaguelu who presented Stew with a three-page document. The document was a government contract for $500,000US and included many seals and official stamps. It had already been signed by the President of Nigeria and the Minister of Education. Dr. Agaguela explained that the government was receiving much oil revenue and that in an effort to develop support from the people of Nigeria, the President had decided to spend some of the money to expand the educational opportunities of its citizens. Bimbola explained that it was important that the contract be signed by Stew and that the necessary payments be made immediately. When Stew asked about how he could pay the necessary "fees" Bimbola told him that he could wire the funds into a bank account, or better yet, Stew "could get cash from his American Express card and be done with it." Bimbola stressed how important he and Dr. Agaguela were in getting this contract, and that many more could follow if Stew took care of them.

Sitting at the table, confused and totally exhausted, Stew wondered what he should do, as he looked at the smiling faces of Bimbola and Dr. Agaguela.

SOURCES

Blauer, E. and J. Laure. (2001). <u>Nigeria</u>. New York: Scholastic.
Nnoromele, S. (2002). <u>Nigeria</u>. San Diego: Lucent.
<u>http://travel.state.gov/tips_nigeria</u>
<u>www.countrywatch.com</u>

This case was prepared by Charles A. Rarick

EXERCISE 10

ARE ETHICS UNIVERSAL?

The Question of Child Labor

Purpose: The purpose of this exercise is to explore the universalist argument for ethical standards, and to develop a better understanding of the ethical dilemmas faced by international managers.

Procedure: Read the background note that follows and then assemble into small groups. Your task to develop a reasoned argument which either attacks or defends child labor.

Background Note:

The International Labor Organization (ILO) estimates that over 250 million children are employed throughout the world, with ages ranging from four to fourteen. A large percentage of these children are employed full-time and do not attend school. Child laborers can be found in large numbers in Africa, Asia, and Latin America. One country known for its child labor is

Pakistan. In Pakistan, carpet master, Sadique, recruits boys ages seven to ten to weave his carpets. Sadique states: "They make ideal employees. Boys at this stage of development are at the peak of their dexterity and endurance, and they're wonderfully obedient." The carpet master can hire a child for about one-fourth the cost of an adult carpet weaver.

Critics of child labor, which includes many international organizations, argue that these children are exploited by their employers, forced to work long hours in poor and dangerous conditions, and are deprived of an opportunity for a better life. They argue that a universal standard should be agreed to by all nations that ensures that no child will be subjected to full-time employment before the age of fourteen.

Others argue that while child labor is never a country's first choice, it is necessary for the survival of some less developed countries. Critics of international standards argue that what is unethical in one country may not be unethical in another. This relativist perspective maintains that child labor standards cannot be applied globally because the economies of the world are not equal. While prosperous countries can afford to keep children in school for a long time, it is necessary that these children work in poorer countries. They point out that rich countries today, such as the United States, had children working during their less prosperous times. It is further argued that without employment, many of these children would be homeless and subject to even greater exploitation on the streets. The families of the working children depend on them in many cases for money for food. The question is not education or work, but rather, work or starvation.

The carpet master in Pakistan quote is from J. Silvers, The Atlantic Monthly, February, 1996.

CPSIA information can be obtained at www.ICGtesting.com
Printed in the USA
LVOW11s1032050915

452914LV00001B/30/P